# A Pocket Guide to
# ROSES

# A Pocket Guide to
# ROSES

## SPECIES, CARE AND GARDEN DESIGN

By Sandra Lindner
Photographs by Jürgen Becker

Bath · New York · Singapore · Hong Kong · Cologne · Delhi · Melbourne

This is a Parragon Book. Copyright © 2008.
Parragon Books Ltd, Queen Street House,
4 Queen Street, Bath BA1 1HE, UK

ISBN 978-1-4075-3017-8
Printed in China

Text: Sandra Lindner.  Photos: Jürgen Becker

Layout, Typography, Composition, Illustration Processing,
Lithography, Editing: Makro Chroma Werbeagentur, Hilden

English-language edition produced by
Cambridge Publishing Management Ltd
Translation: Catherine Landenberger, Gray Sutherland
Project editor: Diane Teillol.  Typesetter: Julie Crane
Copy-editor: Penny Isaac.  Proof-reader: Karolin Thomas
Indexer: Marie Lorimer

# CONTENTS

# ALL THE BASICS
# ABOUT ROSES

# A BRIEF EXCURSION INTO THE WORLD OF BOTANY

## The name of the rose

Garden roses can be divided into two broad categories, wild roses and cultivars. They fit into the botanical nomenclature as follows. All roses belong to the **family** Rosaceae. Next, as a subdivision of the family, they belong to the **genus** *Rosa*. All wild roses come in a wide variety of shapes and sizes and with a range of characteristics. They are then divided into **species**, such as *Rosa canina*, the common dog rose. A new rose is given a **variety** name, regardless of its origin. Varieties of wild rose, which still have much in common with the wild rose in its pure state, are described by their botanical name, such as *Rosa canina* 'Kiese'. The hybrids—and these are by far the majority of our cultivated yard roses—come into being from crossing different varieties of wild roses with each other, wild roses with cultivars, or cultivars with cultivars. The results are then assigned their own names, such as 'Peace'. Variety names may vary from one country to another: as a result, we have synonyms for the same rose. For example, 'Peace', as it is known in the United States, is known as 'Gloria Dei' in Germany and 'Gioia' in Italy. Variety names are of crucial importance to rose lovers, because that is how the plants are listed in the literature, as well as in the rose catalogs.

## Trademarks and registered variety names

Growers often protect the names of new varieties and the "products"—the varieties themselves—in order to remain commercially successful. These two measures are separate. A trademark protects the name of the plant, and can be recognized by the symbol ® following the variety name. Variety name registration is internationally uniform. It grants the grower the sole right to propagate, market, and license the variety for commercial purposes. The first three letters of most registered variety names refer to the grower. For example, the registered variety name of the English Rose 'Heritage' is AUSblush, which indicates its grower, Austin. For most rose lovers, however, trademarks and registered variety names are of little significance.

## Rose blossoms: a world of wonders

While many wild roses bloom only once, cultivars have a wide variety of flowering rhythms.

There are remontant roses, which have a second, albeit rather weak, fall flush;

**PAGES 6–7**
The climber 'New Dawn' earning its reputation as 'Queen of Flowering Plants' in charming fashion by this wrought-iron arbor.

**LEFT**
A group of fragrant, half-open blossoms of the climber 'Arndt'. They will flower again in the fall.

A rose carpet comprising the full blossoms of 'Queen of Denmark', the white blossoms of 'Winchester Cathedral®', the pink blossoms of 'Louise Odier', and the delicate wild roses *Rosa glauca* (center) and *Rosa micrantha* (bottom).

varieties that flower continuously in rich clusters; and long-lasting varieties that remain in bloom from June until first frost, with the occasional, brief pause to catch their breath. The shape and type of blossom are also quite definitely part of the charm of a rose. These range from single blossoms with between five and ten petals; half-filled blossoms with 10 to 20 petals; full blossoms with 20 to 40 petals, all the way to densely filled blossoms with over 40 petals. Beside the number of petals, their form, size, and arrangement also help give each individual blossom its own individual form, be it square, globular, goblet-shaped, rosette-shaped, star-shaped, carnation-shaped, flat, or just plain elegant.

## Fragrance—the soul of the rose

The fragrance of the rose too is mainly located in the blossom. Each fragranced rose has its own body odor, so to speak, which is not merely fleeting but also dependent on temperature and relative humidity, the time of day, and the soil. The fragrance is primarily sited in the corolla, from where it flows from minuscule glands on the upper side of the petals. No wonder, therefore, that densely filled blossoms have a stronger fragrance than single, or that thick petals have a more intense fragrance than wafer-thin. What is more, red and pink roses tend to have the typical rose fragrance, while the fragrance of white and yellow varieties can often resemble that of irises, violets, or lemons, while that of orange roses can be like clover or fruit. Yet even the typical rose fragrance has its varieties and its preferences: in the East people tend to favor the heavy scent of the damask rose, whereas in Grasse, the perfume capital of southern France, people prefer the sweet, delicate smell of Centifolia and the Apothecary's rose.

These large, round, fleshy hips are typical of rugosa hybrids, and have various uses in the kitchen. As with 'Germanica', the long calyx leaves on other rugosa varieties point sharply downward.

### "No rose without thorns"

Although thoroughly well known, in botanical terms this old saying is wrong twice over. First, roses don't have thorns at all, they have spines. Anyone who has removed the spines from a young shoot knows that they are growths that sit on the outside of the shoot and can be removed relatively easily. Real thorns, on the other hand, such as those in a cactus, are part of the core tissue of the plant and are inseparable from it. And the old saying that all roses have spines is also wrong: there are several species that are virtually or entirely spine free. What is more, the spines on the roses that do have them tend to reflect the individuality of each variety: there are hooked spines, straight spines, needle-thin spines, and broad, flat spines—not to mention both hairy and bristly ones.

### Hips—the fruit of the rose

The hips that appear on many roses in late summer come as a surprise, because densely flowered varieties are certainly often sterile. A rosehip is an aggregate fruit formed through the swelling of the calyx beneath the corolla, which contains seeds (small nuts) that ripen within it. The number and size of the seeds depend on the species and variety of rose, as do the shape and color of the hip, which can be globular, flat or round, oval, pear-shaped, spindle-shaped, and bottle-shaped (there are also transitional forms between one and another of these). The outer skin of a rosehip also varies from smooth and bare (the most common form) to covered, with whorls, thistles, or short, thick spines, or as if covered with hoarfrost.

# THE CLASSIFICATION OF ROSES— ORGANIZATION OF THE BOOK

**This book follows the standard classification of roses**
The primary aim of this book is to create a guide to help readers to find their way when negotiating the complex world of the rose, and to include a representative selection of beautiful, robust roses. For this reason, the book follows the standard international criteria for the classification of roses, in a way meaningful to the gardener.

The unusually long, wing-shaped spines on this winged thorn rose (*Rosa sericea* ssp. *omeiensis f. pteracantha*) are endlessly fascinating.

**Old roses:** Chapter 1 (p. 24) discusses Old or Historic roses, not just for chronological reasons, but also because Old roses, with their old-fashioned charm and fragrance, are once again claiming the gardener's attention. It introduces the reader to a number of charming, reliable old favorites, an example of which can be found on the double-page spread on pp. 26–7.

**Modern roses:** In the second half of the 19th century, the era of the Old rose came to an end, and that of the Modern rose began. While Old roses are classified according to how they are related to each other, Modern roses, with their often long, complicated pedigrees, in which species, variety, and group all come together in dizzying fashion, are grouped by species, together with the appropriate organizing possibilities. After Old roses, therefore, the book deals with Modern roses in a series of different chapters: Climbers (p. 58), Shrub Roses (p. 92), Bedding and Border Roses (p. 136), Small Shrub Roses (p. 194), and Miniature Roses (p. 216).

**Wild roses:** Although wild roses are the genetic bedrock from which all species and varieties originally spring, they are used increasingly rarely in the yard. Most of them flower only once, and briefly, and their flowers are modest, though still lovely. The final chapter (Wild Roses, p. 236) limits itself to a small selection of roses, grouping them by their place of origin.

Although *Rosa sweginzowii* 'Macrocarpa' is grown for its decorative hips, its formidable prickles, though they come in many different sizes, make it a defensive paladin beside the ivy.

# TIPS ON CHOOSING AND BUYING ROSES

### How roses are sold

As far as possible, roses should be bought in the form that is most suitable for the planting season.

**Bare-root plants** can be found in rose and tree nurseries in the spring and the fall.

Because roses are basically dug up in the fall and then kept in a controlled environment, they grow best if they are planted between mid-October and mid-November, or in March and April. If planted in September, roses that have been freshly dug up may not have matured enough and may suffer frost damage during the winter. By contrast, if planted in May when the temperature is

Not just an enchanting long bloomer, this bedding rose 'Sommerwind®' also won a prestigious ADR quality certificate.

already fairly warm, roses that have been kept artificially dormant may suffer shock. Bare-root plants should be planted or potted immediately after purchase.

**Pre-packed roses** are available wrapped either in a foil bag or in a plastic container in which their roots are embedded in moisture-retaining material such as moss, potting soil, etc. The canes have sometimes been allowed to grow to limit evaporation to a large extent. This is the form in which roses are often put on sale in home and garden centers. Their chances of taking root are very good. Take care only if the plants have already formed long, pale canes in the container. Nor should the wax layer be removed, because it can easily break through new shoots.

**Roses with a formed root ball** are sold in nets or cellulose containers, which decompose, so they do not have to be removed before planting. Usually, though, the plastic wrapping is removed before planting. In this medium, plants are already active and may already have produced canes. Also, because they are planted without their roots being disturbed, the growth process is not interrupted. Root-ball

### ROSE ASSOCIATIONS

To obtain information and advice about their roses or prospective purchases, rose lovers around the world have a variety of organizations to which they can refer. These range from their local nurseryman to their provincial, state, or national rose society, to the World Federation of Rose Societies (*www.worldrose.org/*). Some of these bodies conduct rose trials of their own, while others maintain registers of varieties. All, however, offer a full program of events for the rose enthusiast. In the US and Canada, the member bodies are the American Rose Society (*www.ars.org*) and the Canadian Rose Society (*www.canadianrosesociety.org*).

In order to enjoy your roses' extravagant splendor and fragrance, you should take care to buy robust, healthy varieties. Here, by an obelisk, the 8-ft. (2.5-m.) climber 'Pink Cloud' displays its most charming side.

roses can be planted up until the end of May. Try to keep a good portion of the soil with the root ball.

**Container roses** can be planted year-round, except when there is frost. Because they already produce fine roots when in the container, they can even be planted in summer. In summer, container roses also have the advantage that the color and shape of their flowers can be seen. These roses should have been container grown and have spread their roots throughout the container. Roses that are put in containers briefly during the summer and have not yet developed a root ball are not really container-grown roses and do not merit the higher price tag. When looking at container roses, take a careful look at the canes and the leaves. The canes should be green and firm and without blemishes, and show no signs of shriveling. The leaves should not be curled or blemished or furred.

### Grading roses

The German Nursery Association (ADR) has issued criteria designed to assist both experts and laypeople by providing practical guidelines for ordering or choosing roses. Grade A shrub roses must have strongly branching roots and no fewer than three strong canes, at least two of which must be growing from the budding union. The third cane may start no more than 2 in. (5 cm.) above. Grade B shrub roses, too, must have strongly branching roots and at least two canes growing from the budding union. When buying stem roses you should make quite certain that they have strong canes growing from at least two buds; this will ensure that the crown grows symmetrically. Crowns growing from only a single bud will tend to be lopsided.

A window curtained with flowers: the giant blossoms of large-flowered climbers 'New Dawn' and 'Alba Meidiland®'. Roses only do well this close to the house if they are not placed under the eaves or in the heat of the midday sun.

# THE RIGHT PLACE TO PLANT ROSES

**What roses need**

If planted in the wrong place, even the healthiest and most robust rose will become sickly and not flower properly. Roses will come into their full glory only if they are planted in a situation that meets their needs. This "situation" includes such factors as climate, position, temperature, soil, light, and air. **Light:** Roses like warm places in sun or half shade. Hollows where cold air gathers or shady positions should be avoided. **Air:** Roses like being where the air and wind can play around them. They suffer in drafty corners and corridors, or places exposed to strong winds. **Soil:** The soil should be loose to a considerable depth (a rose's long taproots tend to suffer in waterlogged soil) and well oxygenated. Roses thrive in loam that is rich in humus and nutrients and has a pH value between 6.2 and 7.1, although to some extent they do tolerate slightly chalky and acid soils. In heavy, compact, marshy soil, or sandy soils, some wild roses may still thrive, perhaps, but not Modern roses. If you must plant roses in such soils, you will have to treat the soil too.

**Making problem soil fit for roses**

Waterlogged, compact soil needs to have the water in it drained away. To improve its permeability, the planting hole needs to be dug deep and wide and the planting soil needs to have compost mixed in with it. Sandy soils, on the other hand, are dry and poor in humus and other nutrients. Their retention capabilities can be enhanced by adding compost and peat as well as a handful of bentonite in each planting hole. (Bentonite is a clayey stone meal rich in trace elements and capable of retaining its own weight in water. It also promotes the formation of humus.) Finally, apply a fine layer of humus mulch. Marshy soil is not suitable for roses. Instead of spending years trying to correct the soil, the thing to do would be to plant a rhododendron or heathland garden.

## Rose-sick soil

If you want to plant new roses in a bed that has already contained other roses or members of the rose family, you will inevitably make an unpleasant new acquaintance. Your newly planted roses will not do well, their shoots will be weak, their leaves few and small, and their flowers few—if any at all. Although roses can thrive for decades in the same soil, when new roses are placed in that soil, the phenomenon known as rose sickness or replant disease soon rears its ugly head. It is suspected that the origins of rose sickness lie in toxic secretions left behind by the former plant's roots, or perhaps also in an accumulation of ray fungus and nematodes. Consequently, you should never plant a new rose in soil in which other roses have been grown. Perhaps it has a parallel in everyday life: when moving into a new house or apartment, often the first thing that people do is to try to get rid of all traces of the previous occupiers. This approach may be the wisest course as far as roses are concerned. When planting roses in an old rose bed, after removing the old rootstock you should dig out the soil from the entire bed down to a depth of about 24 in. (60 cm.) and replace it with fresh soil, perhaps from your vegetable bed, mixed in with compost, or spread with rose potting soil from the nursery. Your roses will thank you for it.

In half shade, the delicate pink blossoms of 'New Dawn' will keep their mother-of-pearl shimmer for ages.

# PLANTING ROSES PROPERLY

**Preparing the soil**
It is always advisable to prepare the soil a few days before planting roses in new beds or on their own. The soil should be dry and frost-free. After removing the grass sward, dig down to about 18 in. (45 cm.). If the soil is heavy, fork it down a little deeper, and then mix the planting soil with sand and compost. In light, sandy soils, on the other hand, it is advisable to work in some compost and bentonite. When refilling the hole, carefully remove all weed roots from the soil. It is essential to do so because otherwise they will create havoc in the rose bed later.

In combination with lavender, the Polyantha 'Ballerina' makes for an artistic setting over 3 ft. (1 m.) high. .

**Planting bare-root shrub roses**
If the roses cannot be planted immediately because it is raining, the ground is frozen, or you simply do not have the time, then heel them in by burying them horizontally under 4 in. (10 cm.) of soil so that the roots and canes do not dry out, and sprinkle water over them to keep the ground damp. Before planting, immerse the rose for at least five hours. During this time the planting hole can be dug out. If the soil has been prepared beforehand, a hole 12 × 12 in. (30 × 30 cm.) will be sufficient, but otherwise, for instance when planting the rose as a single plant in the lawn, it will need to be 20 × 20 in. (50 × 50 cm.). Before placing the plant in the hole, prune the plant and the roots in order to cut damaged or lazy roots back to healthy tissue, and to trim overlong roots to the same length as the others. When doing so, take care not to damage or remove the capillary roots through which the rose draws nutrition. At the same time, trim the canes: on climbers and shrub roses cut them back to

When planting a splendid weeping standard such as 'Raubritter' from bare root, first place a stake in the soil. When planting it in a container, first put a stake in to replace the support provided.

16 in. (40 cm.) and on bedding and large-flowered roses to 6 in. (15 cm.). Now place the rose in the planting hole so that the budding union is 2 in. (5 cm.) lower than the soil level and the roots are vertical. Fill the hole with a mixture of soil and compost and shake the rose gently to ensure that the mixture fills any gaps. Then tread the soil down lightly around the rose so that a slight lip remains, and water copiously. Finally, mound the soil up around the canes together to a height of about 8 in. (20 cm.) to protect the plant against evaporation (this is called "earthing up"). When planting in the fall, leave the earthed-up soil through the winter for protection. When planting in the spring, earthing up is not necessary if fresh new leaves are growing on the stems.

### Planting large-flowered climbers against trees
Instead of felling old trees in your yard, you can use them as the most wonderful supports for climbing roses. The best trees for this are apples and pears that have long since passed their prime, but old white cedars and deep-rooted conifers such as larch and Scotch pine are also perfectly suitable. There are two ways of doing this.

Close planting: Using a pickax, dig a trench 24 × 24 × 24 in. (60 × 60 × 60 cm.) deep about 24 in. (60 cm.) away from the trunk and mix a good amount of compost together with the soil from the trench. Next, knock the bottom out of a pail and place that in the trench, and then plant the rose with its roots within the sides of the pail. This will help to protect the rose roots from competing for nutrients with the tree roots. Once the rose is growing canes, tie the canes securely to the tree trunk and train them into the branches.

Planting at a distance: If the tree has very dense foliage and casts a lot of shade, plant the rose outside its perimeter. Lean a tall stepladder against the tree at an angle and train the canes up it, securing them to it.

# THE ROSE GARDENER'S CARE CALENDAR

## Spring

**February:** Use brushwood or reed matting to protect roses in exposed positions from the winter sun. As this is a quieter time of year as far as gardening is concerned, you may want to study rose catalogs and draw up planting plans. **March:** New roses can be planted as soon as the ground is frost-free. Toward the middle of the month, remove the protective matting and covering from climbing roses. At the end of March, remove the soil that was used for earthing up and spread it among the roses. Dig and weed the soil. After the last frost, fertilize the soil with rose fertilizer. **April:** Dig and weed the soil again and do the main pruning. In addition, the roses can also receive special rose mulch.

## Early and mid-summer

**May:** Dig those rose beds that have not been mulched once more. Check new shoots regularly for pests and disease and remove and destroy affected areas as soon as they appear. Spray species liable to fungus infection with fungicide. Remove suckers from the base. Tie vigorous new shoots on climbers to their supports to encourage upright growth. If you only use long-lasting organic fertilizers, now is the time to apply them. **June:** Fertilize the roses once more before the first flowers open. In extended dry conditions, water. Tie long climber canes again. Keep vigorous bushes such as Ladies' Mantle (*Alchemilla*) and geraniums under control, so they do not encroach too much on the roses. Check roses regularly for pests and disease. Remove affected areas and spray as required. **July:** Deadhead recurrent bloomers regularly. The correct place to cut is just above the first fully formed leaf under the dead head. If, however, you want the hips, do not deadhead the roses. From mid-July on, do not apply any more nitrogenous fertilizer so that the canes will mature and become hardy for the winter. Check roses regularly for pests and disease. Remove affected areas and spray as required.

The pink blossoms of 'Mevrouw Nathalie Nypels' have an almost whitish gleam.

In June and July many yard gates open invitingly on to rose blossoms. Here visitors are welcomed at the gate by three climbers: (left to right) 'Paul Transon', 'Chaplin's Pink Climber', and 'New Dawn'.

## Late summer and fall

**August:** Start summer pruning of one-time flowering climbers (see p. 61). Water in dry conditions. This is the season when black spot widely appears. Remove affected leaves, also from the ground. Spray as required. Deadhead recurrent bloomers regularly.
**September:** Hoe and remove weeds. Early in the month, apply patentkali to recurrent bloomers (approximately 1½ oz. per square yard/40 g. per square meter). This will harden the wood and make it hardy for the winter. Keep vigorous neighboring bushes under control.
**October:** Begin planting. Roses can now be transplanted. Harvest hips.

## Winter care

The canes on climbers on freestanding supports and in exposed positions need to be protected from wind, sun, and frost. Collect all the leaves from the ground that have fallen from the canes. Earth up around the base of the canes to a height of about 12 in. (30 cm.) and wrap the canes in sacking, bamboo, reed, or straw matting. **November:** New planting can continue. At the end of the month, trim shrub roses slightly to avoid snow breakage, and remove the leaves from the ground. Remove the leaves from bedding and large-flowered roses and then earth up. Cut back the upper canes by about one-third. **December:** Wrap climbers over arches in reed or bamboo matting for protection. Earth up recurrent bloomers. Cover bedding and large-flowering varieties with reeds. Take bucket roses into the garage, or place them on thick Styrofoam matting in a sheltered place and wrap them in sacking or bubble wrap. Water on frost-free days. Protect the head and budding union on taller stems with reed matting or jute sacking. **January:** In case of heavy snowfall, tie shrub roses loosely together to avoid snow breakage.

However charming the intertwining of climbers such as 'Pink Cloud' and clematis such as 'Hagley Hybrid' may be, when they become too bushy the roses may become prone to fungal infestation.

# ROSE DISEASES

**Rose leaves as target surface**

The most common diseases affecting roses are fungal infestations. Unfortunately, they cannot always be attributed to a poor choice of planting position, incorrect treatment, or susceptible variants. The weather also plays a large role. These infections mainly affect the leaves, the organs through which roses breathe and digest and which determine if they will thrive or perish. According to the nature of the attack, leaf diseases may lead to inhibited growth or even to the death of the plant. One of the most stubborn and insidious leaf diseases is black spot.

**Black spot**

**Symptoms:** This common leaf disease most frequently strikes in late summer and fall, but can also appear in June if the weather is sunny. It appears as rounded violet to black spots with jagged edges. It usually starts by attacking the lower leaves first. The leaf yellows and then falls off. If not treated quickly, it can lead to complete leaf loss and death of the plant. **Cause:** Infection of leaves and soil in cold, damp weather. **Prevention:** Spray susceptible varieties early in the year with a strengthening compound. Watch air conditions and apply sufficient patentkali. **Remedies:** Remove affected leaves from the plant and the soil below. Spray with commercially available fungicides at intervals of ten to fourteen days.

**Genuine mildew**
**Symptoms:** Fair weather fungus that appears when the temperature rises above 68°F (20°C) and the relative humidity is also high, as early as June. A white, powdery deposit forms on young growth such as shoots, buds, sepals, and the tops of leaves. It is easily wiped off. Later the leaves crumple and turn red, but do not fall off. The wood weakens and the rose becomes prone to frost damage. **Cause:** Warm, damp

The fragrant climber 'May Queen' likes a position with good air circulation by a pergola or in trees. If planted by a wall it may suffer.

weather, inadequate air circulation, unbalanced fertilization. **Prevention:** Avoid nitrogenous fertilizers. Choose planting positions with good air circulation. In the fall, cut back affected parts to healthy tissue. **Remedies:** Remove affected parts. Spray with commercially available fungicides.

**False mildew**
**Symptoms:** White deposit on the undersides of leaves. Dark spots on the tops of leaves. Affected leaves wither and fall off. In contrast to black spot, attacks plants downward, upper parts first. **Cause:** Large variations in temperature in late summer and fall, leaving dew on the leaves. This creates ideal conditions for fungus, especially in sheltered positions. **Prevention:** Choose positions that are sunny and not too confined, with good air circulation, so that roses can dry out properly. **Remedies:** Remove affected canes and leaves. Spray with commercially available fungicides.

**Rose rust**
**Symptoms:** Pin-sized, orange, spore traces on the undersides of leaves in early summer. Small yellowish spots on the tops of leaves. In fall, black pustules on the undersides of leaves, leading to leaves falling and weakening of plant. **Cause:** Infection during warm weather, also during dry weather. Usually affects specific varieties. **Prevention:** Adequate Patentkali treatment. Choose planting positions with good air circulation. Loosen the soil. **Remedies:** Remove affected parts. Treat with rose-rust spray. Also spray the undersides of leaves and neighboring plants. Alternate products.

PLANT YOUR OWN NEIGHBORHOOD WATCH
You can help protect your roses by planting companion species that are hostile to fungus and other pests, such as garlic, allium, onions, chives, sage (*Salvia officinalis*), lavender (*Lavandula angustifolia*), tagetes (*Tagetes*), wormwood, artemisia, and marigold (*Calendula officinalis*).

# ROSE PESTS

**Greenfly (aphids)**
**Symptoms:** Greenfly cluster and feed on new shoots, buds, and leaves. Leaves and flowers become stunted. Greenfly may transfer viruses, black ascomycetes, to the sticky matter exuded. **Causes:** Serious over-fertilizing with nitrogenous fertilizer. Hot, dry positions favor infestation. **Remedies:** Spray with a solution of spirit and soft soap. Heavy rain can reduce infestation. Only spray with commercial preparations in extreme situations.

**Red spider mite**
**Symptoms:** Infestation, often very intense, in hot, dry conditions, starting in May. Climbers against south-facing walls are particularly at risk. Minute orange-red mites, visible only under a magnifying glass, that cluster and feed on the undersides of leaves. Leaf tops turn brownish yellow, and then the leaves fall. **Cause:** Hot, dry weather. **Remedies:** Spray with acaricide. Use predatory mites for biological control.

**Leaf-rolling sawfly**
**Symptoms:** Rose leaves roll up like cigars. **Cause:** The rolled-up leaves contain leaf-rolling sawfly eggs. In July the larvae abandon the leaves and pupate in the soil. **Remedy:** Remove affected leaves regularly. Spraying is not necessary.

The apricot-colored blossoms of 'Cressida', an English rose, have an enchanting fragrance.

To the eye, roses and lavender are not exactly a dream couple, as the English rose 'Mary Rose®' and the lavender variety 'Munstead' clearly show. But the components of lavender's scent keep aphids away from roses.

## Leafhopper
**Symptoms:** Fine, white, mosaic-like mottling on the tops of leaves. On the undersides, greenish, slender, jumping insects that feed along the leaf veins. **Cause:** Common on climbers grown against warm walls and in other hot, dry places. **Remedy:** Spray leaf tops and undersides with commercially available insecticides.

## Thrips
**Symptoms:** Stunted flowers, silverish spots on leaves and petals. Tapping flowers brings out tiny, slender, jumping bugs. **Cause:** Hot, dry weather from June on. **Remedies:** Cut off badly affected buds and flowers. Spray with commercial insecticides.

## Rose-shoot sawfly
**Symptoms:** Individual shoot points stunted. **Cause:** Sawfly larvae eat their way into the medulla. Downward-boring sawflies lay their eggs in the points of shoots. The larvae bore downward into the shoot and continue to eat down. Upward-boring sawflies lay their eggs in leaf stalks. The larvae bore upward into the shoot, eating it. **Remedies:** Search carefully for affected shoots and cut back to healthy wood. Kill the larvae. Spraying is not necessary.

## Rose slug-worm
**Symptoms:** Moth-eaten leaves, until all that remains are transparent, parchment-like areas. **Cause:** The green larvae of the rose slug-worm (a small, black sawfly) eat the parts of leaves that contain chlorophyll. **Remedy:** Destroy affected leaves along with the caterpillars.

# OLD
# ROSES

# OLD ROSES

## What exactly are Old roses?

The name Old or Historic roses is used to describe yard roses that evolved through coincidence, mutation, or neglect in the nursery before the first hybrid Teas. They are

grouped together by phylogenetic origin and relationship. The typical classification by appearance is only possible with some roses, and then only by certain qualities. What all Old roses have in common are their colors, which are silky to velvety and always soft, never loud or gaudy; the shape of their blooms, which are usually densely filled and old-fashioned; and

There is evidence that the Damask rose 'Celsiana', with its delightful fragrance, was cultivated even before 1750. This variety is also suitable for planting as a hedge.

their intoxicating fragrance. Delicate colors predominate, although there are also white, burgundy, and deep purple varieties. Pure yellow and scarlet are also missing, as is the repeat-blooming ability that Modern roses have. Because of these typical qualities, there is a tendency nowadays to understand—and use—the description "Old roses" as a feature of a given style of rose.

Until the 18th century, virtually all the roses in Europe flowered just once, as did wild roses and the old yard roses that already existed back then, such as Alba, Gallica, Damask, Centifolia, and Moss roses. They were undemanding, healthy, winter-hardy plants that thrived even in half shade. In about 1750, people started to cross imported China roses, thereby creating the remontant (i.e. reblooming in fall) groups of Noisette, Portland, Bourbon, and remontant roses. As a rule, however, these are less hardy and more prone to leaf diseases.

**PAGES 24–5**
The Old rose category also includes varieties in which all the best qualities combine, such as healthy foliage, beautiful growth, and fine, fragrant, recurrent blooms. 'Jacques Cartier' (see previous page, and p. 34), 'Rose de Resht' (p. 33), 'Stanwell Perpetual' (p. 38), 'Mme Isaac Pereire' (p. 52), and 'Souvenir de la Malmaison' (p. 52) are all Old roses.

**FALLING PETALS**
However romantic and perfect densely filled rose blooms seem to be, they also need great care when they blossom. If falling petals land on the leaves beneath them, and continue to lie there, they are quick to attract gray mould, especially when it rains. So remove petals from leaves regularly.

'Celsiana' (front) and 'Trigintipetala' (rear) Damask roses splash about with globe thistles (*Echinops ritro*, behind) and white foxglove (*Digitalis purpurea* 'Alba') among flattened yew cones.

## Pruning once-flowering Old roses

When it comes to the groups, normal pruning to retain the shape of the plant is not needed if you have so much space available that the flowers can be allowed to spread happily and naturally along their arching, bowed canes. Nonetheless, canes that have become too old should be pruned at the end of March every second or third year. Varieties that tend to fall apart or that simply only need to offer a pleasing aspect in the yard should be pruned hard, shortly before flowering starts in late May/early June, to give them shape. At this point, the bushes will have already produced two types of shoots: budding shoots and vegetative shoots. The latter tend to detract from the closed form of the rose and may even cover the flowers, so they need to be cut back just below the level of the flowers. In this way, the rose not only retains its compact, beautiful shape but may also provide the flowers with even more energy. If the roses have to fit compactly in a combination with other perennials, all the shoots should be cut back by one or two feet and then pruned. This does, however, reduce the quantity of flowers. Instead of blossoming on arching, bowed branches, they will now merely sit just above the leaves.

## Pruning repeat-blooming Old roses

China, Portland, Bourbon, and remontant roses should be pruned hard from the first year after being planted so they will bush out nicely. The shape to strive for is to keep the sides down and let the bush grow taller as it approaches the center. In this way you will avoid having a bald base. With Portlands, cut back a good half of the new growth. With robust Bourbons and remontants, which are small climbers, cut the new growth back to about 5 or 6 in. (15 cm.). China roses, which are rather weak growers, should be cut back to about half of the previous year's growth.

# 'FÉLICITÉ PARMENTIER'
ALBA ROSE

**FLOWERING:** One-time
  bloomer; very dense;
  mussel pink at the center,
  lightening toward the edge;
  Ø about 3 in. (8 cm.);
  delightful fragrance
**GROWTH:** 3½–5½ ft.
  (1–1.5 m.) high; bushy;
  arching; compact;
  closed form
**FEATURES:** Robust climber;
  very winter hardy; tolerates
  half shade and relatively
  poor soil
**PLANTING:** Bedding rose;
  also for fences and hedges,
  and to edge wooded areas
**INTRODUCED:** Parmentier,
  1836, France

The origins of this delicate beauty are completely
unknown. It first appeared in about 1836 and ever since
has captivated with the opulence and delightful fragrance
of its flowers, which open in June from large clusters
of yellowish round buds above the leaves. The pale,
blush-pink flowers develop from almost globular shells
to a grand, flat, almost creamy-white rosette, in which
the inner corolla is closely folded, producing a sort of
green eye at the center of the flower. What we have here
is a merging of styles, a quality typical of quite a number
of Old roses. Flowering is so long and luxuriant that the
canes tend to bend over and therefore must be supported.

# 'MME PLANTIER'

Synonym: 'Madame Plantier' / ALBA ROSE

"I like to look at it in moonlight," Vita Sackville-West wrote of 'Madame Plantier', "It glows beside the old apple tree like a pear-shaped ghost." She had planted a 'Madame Plantier' to climb into an apple tree in her yard; eventually it grew until it was 46 ft. (14 m.) around.

At first creamy-white and later pure-white flowers appear in great clusters from pointed, rose-red tinted buds at the end of long, almost prickle-free canes from June to July. As a bush, it grows loosely, its canes hanging over, and needs support to give it shape. As a climber, too, it needs to be firmly secured. Its loose growing pattern and long canes would tend to suggest that this is no pure Alba rose.

▶ 'Semiplena' (synonyms: 'White Rose of York', 'Bonnie Prince Charlie's Rose') is another white Alba rose that was very popular as long ago as the Middle Ages. It is a powerful shrub rose growing to nearly 7 ft. (2 m.), which produces a rich display of fragrant, half-full flowers followed by large red hips.

**FLOWERING:** Once-flowering; dense; irregular; Ø about 3 in. (8 cm.); creamy white; gentle fragrance

**GROWTH:** Up to 8 × 8 ft. (2.5 × 2.5 m.); 20 ft. (5 m.) and over as a climber

**FEATURES:** Winter hardy climber, suits half shade and northern exposures

**PLANTING:** As a climber, very attractive on pillars, obelisks, arches, bowers, and in trees; as a bush, suits large yards and being near water

**INTRODUCED:** Plantier, 1835, France

# 'KÖNIGIN VON DÄNEMARK'

ALBA ROSE / Synonyms: 'Queen of Denmark', 'New Maiden Blush', 'Naissance de Vénus'

**FLOWERING:** Once-flowering; very dense; quartered; with a green eye; flat; Ø about 2½ in. (6 cm.); warm rose color; intoxicating fragrance

**GROWTH:** Up to 5 ft. (1.5 m.) high; upright; compact

**FEATURES:** Robust climber; very winter hardy; also thrives in half shade

**PLANTING:** Glorious as a backdrop for herbaceous and mixed borders

**INTRODUCED:** Booth, 1816, Germany; on sale since 1826

Many regard this as the most beautiful of all the Alba roses. 'Königin von Dänemark' was created in 1816 in the Flottbek nursery of the Scots-born James Booth as a seedling of 'Maiden's Blush'. When in 1826 he first included it in his catalog, he dedicated it to Princess Marie Sophie Friederike of Hessen-Kassel, the consort of King Frederik VI of Denmark. This should come as no surprise. In those days, Flottbek belonged to Holsten, which in turn was tied to Denmark under a personal union. The rose is a clear favorite among gardeners to this day. Its flowers stand gracefully and easily visible above the bush, opening even in rainy weather to a perfect shape. Even after flowering has ended, the bush, with its decorative foliage, is a jewel.

# 'GREAT MAIDEN'S BLUSH'

Synonyms: 'Cuisse de Nymphe', 'Incarnata', 'La Virginale', 'La Séduisante' / ALBA ROSE

Often represented in Flemish paintings, 'Great Maiden's Blush' is not only one of the oldest European roses but also, as its various names suggest, one of the most beloved and seductive of all roses. In June, the firm, creamy buds at the tips of its canes open into a rich cluster of flowers, which are so heavy that they bend the twigs right over. Since 1797 a smaller variant, 'Small Maiden's Blush' or 'Maiden's Blush, Small', has been available, which is more delicate in growth and flower size than its big sister. It reaches a height of only about 4 ft. (1.2 m.) and can also be grown in large containers. The weakness of its delicate flowers, which tend to decay if exposed to lengthy periods of rain, can be prevented by treating the plant once in April with liquid patentkali (2 oz. per sq. yard/50 g. per sq. meter).

▶ As its synonym 'Céleste' would indicate, the loosely filled pink blossoms of 'Celestial', which appear in June and July, are simply heavenly. 'Celestial', which was already known in the 18th century for its beauty and fragrance, is a shrub rose that grows to about 6 ft. (1.8 m.).

**FLOWERING:** One-time bloomer; dense; pale pink, yellowish at the edge, later almost white; Ø 3 in. (8 cm.); strong fragrance

**GROWTH:** Up to 7 ft. (2 m.) high; strong growth; arching

**FEATURES:** Robust climber; very winter hardy; also thrives in half shade

**PLANTING:** As a specimen in beds and borders, as a hedge; at the edge of a wooded area; or as a climber

**INTRODUCED:** In Europe, 15th century or earlier

# 'MME HARDY'

DAMASK ROSE / Synonym: 'Madame Hardy'

**FLOWERING:** One-time bloomer; very dense; green carpel in the middle; Ø about 3 in. (7 cm.); white; musky fragrance

**GROWTH:** Up to 5 ft. (1.5 m.) high; strong; upright; arching

**FEATURES:** Robust climber; very winter hardy; also thrives in half shade; tolerates poor soil

**PLANTING:** Beside fences, in beds and hedges, also as a climber; thrives in half shade

**INTRODUCED:** Hardy, 1832, France

'Madame Hardy' deserves to be counted among the Old rose classics. This bold, top-class variety is astonishingly adaptable—it is equally at home in elegant city yards, enchanting romantic gardens, among white plants or in colorful country yards. Its long, pointed calyces are particularly striking, towering above the buds; as are later the green, horn-shaped carpels in the midst of its white, identically formed flowers. This green eye is formed from the styles growing together and stands out in strong contrast to the flat, white flowers. Blossoming starts in June and lasts for six weeks; the flowers gradually open in great clusters on the numerous lateral canes as well.

◄ In contrast to 'Madame Hardy', 'Miranda' belongs to the group of remontant Damask roses. Its large, fragrant flowers, which gradually open out into flat blossoms, seem as if created for the ball season.

# 'ROSE DE RESHT'

Synonym: 'Rose de Rescht' / PORTLAND ROSE (often classified as a Damask rose)

'Rose de Resht' is a stunningly beautiful foundling whose origins remain a mystery. In June its firm, round buds open out into delicate, rosette-shaped flowers that usually grow just about the leaves in small clusters and give off an intense, bewitching fragrance. The brilliant color fades to a soft magenta before fading altogether. Young bushes (up to about five years old) continue to bloom until the fall. In older plants, flowering potency drops off until they are hardly remontant any longer. To retain their potency, it is recommended cutting such plants back hard in the spring.

**FLOWERING:** Recurrent; very densely filled, pompon shape; Ø about 2 in. (5 cm.); bright carmine with golden stamens; strong, exotic fragrance

**GROWTH:** Compact upright and powerful; about 3 ft. (90 cm.) high

**FEATURES:** Ideal climber; very winter hardy; also thrives in half shade; tolerates poorer soil

**PLANTING:** For beds, borders, near patios, terraces, paths, as a hedge, ideal for smaller yards; also as a stem rose and in containers

**INTRODUCED:** Discovered by Nancy Lindsay near the city of Resht, in Iran, in 1950

# 'JACQUES CARTIER'

PORTLAND ROSE / Synonym: 'Marquise de Boccella'

**FLOWERING:** Recurrent; densely filled, quartered, large blossoms; Ø 3½ in. (9 cm.); pink, fading to the edge; intense fragrance
**GROWTH:** About 3 ft. (1–1.2 m.) high; arching. Can be pruned to grow upright and compact
**FEATURES:** Robust climber; winter hardy; tolerates half shade and poorer soil
**PLANTING:** Ideal for town gardens, beds, hedges. Easy to grow in containers
**INTRODUCED:** Moreau-Robert, 1868, France

The close relationship between Portland and Damask roses can be clearly seen in the damask bud of the blossoms of 'Jacques Cartier', where the inner petals of the densely filled flowers reflex. 'Jacques Cartier' has other persuasive qualities, though. It has little susceptibility to fungal diseases and flowers twice a year. The first flowering takes place in June, dense clusters emerging from tight, red buds, the second, a little weaker, toward the end of August. Another characteristic of Portland roses is the way the flowers stand on short stems just above the dense foliage. If you want a compact, upright bush, then simply cut the canes back by a third early in the year.

◀ 'The Portland Rose' (synonyms: 'Duchess of Portland', 'Paestana', 'Portlandica') is the ancestor of all the Portland roses and is also remontant, flowering in the fall. The bush, only 36 in. (90 cm.) tall, with its bright red flowers, was first grown in Italy in about 1790.

# 'MME BOLL'

Synonym: 'Madame Boll' / PORTLAND ROSE

Without doubt the best Portland rose, 'Madame Boll', sometimes wrongly confused with 'Comte de Chambord', can look back on a long, successful story. The flowers, which lie directly above the foliage, bloom in all their glory from June to July. Usually, they have a second flush that lasts from the end of August until first frost. The only problem affecting this easy-to-care-for decorative bush is a tendency for its buds not to open if it rains a lot during first flush, but instead for them to ball. The remedy, however, is easy: all the gardener needs to do is remove the stuck outer petals. Should such obstetric assistance not be forthcoming, the blooms will rot unopened on the bush, giving rise to the so-called mummy formation.

**FLOWERING:** Recurrent; very densely filled, quartered, flat; Ø 3½ in. (8 cm.); bright pink, lightening to the edge; intense musky fragrance

**GROWTH:** About 4 ft. (1.2 m.) high; strong; upright; compact

**FEATURES:** Robust climber; very winter hardy; well suited to half shade; tolerates poorer soil

**PLANTING:** Beds, borders, hedges, and containers

**INTRODUCED:** First grown 1843 by Daniel Boll in the USA, sold in Europe by Boyau as 'Madame Boll' since 1859

# 'CHARLES DE MILLS'

GALLICA ROSE / Synonyms: 'Bizarre Triomphante', 'Ardoisée', 'Violette Bronzée'

**FLOWERING:** Single; very densely filled; flat; dark maroon/crimson; large; Ø 4 in. (10 cm.); strong, individual fragrance
**GROWTH:** About 5 ft. (1.5 m.) high; strong; upright; almost as wide as it is tall
**FEATURES:** Robust climber; very winter hardy; well suited to half shade, but needs good soil
**PLANTING:** Suitable for elegant and romantic gardens as well as country gardens; also beds, to edge wooded areas, and as a hedge
**INTRODUCED:** Before 1811, origin unknown

'Charles de Mills' flowers on long canes in clusters above the foliage and is noteworthy not only for its thrilling color but also for the closed, round contours of its densely filled, crimson-maroon blooms, which are often quartered. When planted with blue and mauve flowers such as *Allium* or Old Man's Beard (*Penstemon*) as companions, as well as against silver or gray foliage, it makes for a picturesque yard. In late summer, as with many dark Gallica hybrids, there is a tendency for it to develop mildew. The best remedy is to cut out affected shoots and spray with a fungicide. Before winter, remove all leaves from the soil, because the fungus will winter in them. When all is said and done, however, it cannot seriously harm this robust rose.

# 'CARDINAL DE RICHELIEU'

Synonym: 'Rose Van Sian' / GALLICA ROSE

'Cardinal de Richelieu' is one of the deepest-colored roses. Its blooms open in June, deep maroon against a lighter background. Gradually, the petals reflex from the original cupped calyx until they almost form a ball. At the same time, the color darkens into a deep purple. If the rose is left to its own devices, it will grow into a dense tangle of long, arching, almost thornless canes, with sumptuous flowering. To start the plant flowering it is essential to cut back old canes yearly, right down to the base, to prune the long, bare, vegetative canes back to bush level before the buds open, and early in the spring to give the bush a round shape with tapered sides.

**FLOWERING:** Single; filled; Ø 3 in. (8 cm.); dark maroon/purple; fragrant

**GROWTH:** About 5 ft. (1.5 m.) high; bushy and arching

**FEATURES:** Needs good soil; not for planting in full sun; winter hardy

**PLANTING:** Beds and fences, to edge wooded areas; as a specimen; in hedges; as a climber up bright pillars

**INTRODUCED:** Laffay, 1840, France

▶ At 5 ft. (1.5 m.) high, 'Tuscany' (synonym: 'Black Tuscany') is another Gallica whose velvety blooms have violet to brownish tones. This very winter-hardy rose has a long tradition behind it, being mentioned as long ago as 1597, when it went by the name of 'Old Velvet Rose'.

# 'STANWELL PERPETUAL'
PIMPERNEL ROSE

**FLOWERING:** Perpetual; filled; Ø 1½ in. (4 cm.); bright pink, later creamy white; wonderful fragrance
**GROWTH:** About 5 ft. (1.5 m.) high and 4 ft. (1.2 m.) wide; strong, thick, arching, with very thorny canes
**FEATURES:** Robust climber; very winter hardy; tolerates half shade
**PLANTING:** Beds, hedges, to edge wooded areas, and containers
**INTRODUCED:** Lee, 1838, Great Britain

These enchanting roses probably originated from a chance of nature, and can be traced back to a cross between the Pimpernel rose (*Rosa spinosissima/pimpinellifolia*), which is native to northern Europe, and *Rosa × damascena* 'Bifera'. 'Stanwell Perpetual' is the only Pimpernel that blooms continuously until late fall. With its profusion of seductively fragranced, little mussel-red flowers, it soon became many gardeners' favorite. While Vita Sackville-West loved it because it flowered until October, the grower Heinrich Schultheiss concentrated more on its waterfall-like growth, which destined it for planting as a weeping standard. 'Stanwell Perpetual' looks as artistic when planted in great containers on columns, walls, or posts as it does when ennobled as a long-stem rose.

◄ While 'Stanwell Perpetual' makes an elegant yard variety, the Pimpernel's other descendants have rather more of the flair of a child of nature. The short-lived though brilliant flowers of 'Glory of Edzell' appear in May.

# 'OFFICINALIS'

Synonyms: *Rosa gallica* 'Officinalis', 'Apothecary's rose' / GALLICA ROSE

'Officinalis' is the oldest Gallica. Its name clearly points toward its lengthy historic significance. It probably arrived in Europe at the time of the Crusades, having been brought from the Middle East, where Arab physicians had already discovered its healing properties. Once in Europe, there is evidence that it was being cultivated in Provins (southeast of Paris) in the early 14th century for its rose oil and other medical reasons. Later, it became the emblem of the House of Lancaster and, with the white rose of York (*Rosa alba*) superimposed upon it, forms the Tudor Rose, the traditional heraldic emblem of England. Because its petals retain their fragrance even when dry, 'Officinalis' is also prized for potpourris.

**FLOWERING:** Single; half filled; large; Ø 4 in. (11 cm.); carmine with yellow stamens; heavy, dark fragrance

**GROWTH:** About 3 ft. (1 m) high and 4 ft. (1.2 m.) wide; strong, compact, round arching

**FEATURES:** Bushy winter hardy; well suited to half shade; tolerates poorer soil; good rosehip producer

**PLANTING:** Suitable for small yards, vegetable gardens, and country gardens. Also for beds, hedges, and containers

**INTRODUCED:** Already cultivated by 1310

**OTHER SYNONYMS:** 'Red Rose of Lancaster', 'Common Provins Rose', 'Old Red Damask'

# 'VERSICOLOR'

GALLICA ROSE / Synonyms: 'Fair Rosamond's Rose', 'Rosa Mundi'

'Versicolor' is a sport (a mutant offshoot) of *Rosa gallica* 'Officinalis', which it closely resembles. It is the oldest known streaked rose and was certainly picked out in the Renaissance: it was first described in 1583 (as *Rosa gallica* 'Variegata') by the Flemish botanist Charles de l'Ecluse (Carolus Clusius). In the yard, 'Versicolor' is a very lively and decorative element. As a hedge of flames beside the calm of a gravel or paved path, its effect reaches brilliant heights. Because its flowers also attract bees, 'Versicolor' also produces an abundance of hips. If planted with its original roots (i.e. not as a graft), it tends to produce suckers and then, like a ground-cover rose, may be used to strengthen slopes and banks.

**FLOWERING:** Single; half filled; large; Ø 4 in. (10 cm.); bright carmine, irregular white/pink marbling streaked with yellow stamens; heavy, dark fragrance

**GROWTH:** About 3 ft. (1 m.) high and 4 ft. (1.2 m.) wide; strong, compact, round arching bush

**FEATURES:** Robust climber; very winter hardy; well suited to half shade; tolerates poorer soil; good hip producer

**PLANTING:** Suitable for small yards, vegetable gardens, and country gardens; also for beds, hedges, and containers

**INTRODUCED:** First described in 1583. Originator unknown

▼ The once-flowering 'Georges Vibert' (synonym: 'Gallica Meleagris') is also streaked. With its large, dense flowers and its bushy, upright growth and measuring only just over 3 ft. (1 m.), it is ideal for small yards, containers, and yard niches.

# 'REINE DES CENTFEUILLES'
CENTIFOLIA

**FLOWERING:** Single;
very densely filled; large;
Ø 4 in. (10 cm.); pink;
delicate fragrance
**GROWTH:** About 5 ft.
(1.5 m.) high and up to
3 ft. (1 m.) wide;
upright to arching bush
**FEATURES:** Robust climber;
very winter hardy; tolerates
half shade and poor soil
**PLANTING:** Suitable for beds,
to edge wooded areas, and
containers
**INTRODUCED:** 1824,
Belgium

The fragrance of 'Reine des Centfeuilles', which in a good
year can bloom almost extravagantly, is royal indeed.
In rainy years, on the other hand, its opening blossoms
often run the risk of balling, being unable to open fully
unless the gardener physically removes the outer petals.
Once they have opened, however, they give off an utterly
delightful fragrance and can also be used in a variety of
gourmet food preparations. A complete blossom makes
a captivating cake decoration; individual petals coated
with egg white and sprinkled with icing sugar make very
attractive crystallized decorations for pastries, desserts, or
cheese; and fresh petals can enliven salads with their pink
colors and rose fragrance.

◄ In addition, the Centifolia include even smaller-
blossomed sports such as 'Petite de Hollande', which, at
4 ft. (1.2 m.) high, towers over the others. It has a variety
of other names, including *Rosa × centifolia* 'Minor',
'Petite Junon de Hollande', 'Bordeaux des Dames',
'Gros Pompon', and 'Pompon des Dames'.

# 'PARVIFOLIA'

Synonym: *Rosa centifolia* 'Parvifolia' / CENTIFOLIA

Like all Centifolia, this little one likes a lot of sunshine. In a well-chosen position it is uncommonly generous, flowering with enchanting opulence. Apparently it was discovered in an overgrown Dijon yard and was first described and illustrated in 1664 by Tabernaemontanus as a Burgundy rose. By contrast, 'Parvifolia' flowers in clusters at the end of almost thornless canes, much like a Gallica. It flowers only once, in June, but its flush is very long-lasting and rich.

**FLOWERING:** Single; densely filled; flat; Ø 1½ in. (4 cm.); dark purple with violet tints; ranunculus-like reflexed petals; strong fragrance

**GROWTH:** About 2 ft. (0.6 m.) high; upright, bushy, thick

**FEATURES:** Generous flowering climber; winter hardy

**PLANTING:** Suitable for small yards, low hedges, beds, and containers; good with herbs

**INTRODUCED:** First produced about 1664

# 'NUITS DE YOUNG'

MOSS ROSE / Synonym: 'Old Black'

**FLOWERING:** One-time bloomer; filled, flat rosettes; medium-sized; Ø 2 in. (5 cm.); dark, velvety purple with violet/brown; heavy, intense fragrance

**GROWTH:** About 4 ft. (1.2 m.) high; strong growth, upright, bushy

**FEATURES:** Winter hardy; needs a sunny position

**PLANTING:** Suitable for small yards, low hedges, beds, and containers; very good with herbs

**INTRODUCED:** Laffay, 1845, France

Originally, this darkest of all the Moss roses went by the name 'Old Black', because of its deep color. On slightly mossy stems and from equally mossy buds, blooms open in June whose color ranges from chestnut brown to purple, softening later to a charming deep lilac that creates a vivid contrast with the yellow stamens. Because dark-colored flowers rarely produce any great effect from a distance, this plant—and its enchanting fragrance—need to be enjoyed from close by. Recommended planting positions therefore would be in a sunny part of a patio or seating area. There the fragrance will be at its fullest and the rose can also be combined with other fragrant plants such as lavender, pinks, and sage.

◄ The moss on the calyx of 'Cristata' (synonyms: 'Chapeau de Napoléon', 'Crested Moss'), which recalls Napoleon's three-cornered hat, is particularly attractive. Its huge, heavy flowers will need supporting, though.

# 'MUSCOSA'

Synonym: 'Centifolia Muscosa' / ORIGINAL MOSS ROSE

'Muscosa' is a sport from *Rosa × centifolia*. Its stems and calyx are covered with fine moss (actually, a mutation of the glands that creates the impression of mossing). The sticky resin from the glands combines with the sweet Centifolia fragrance to produce a very special scent. Other mutations are often sold as 'Muscosa' roses. With the same height, about 4 ft. (1.2 m.), while more stable and more pleasing in shape, they go by other names in England, such as 'Old Pink Moss', 'Common Moss', or 'Communis'. There is also a white variant, known as 'Muscosa Alba' (also 'White Moth', 'White Bath', or 'Clifton Moss'), and yet another, a purple variant known as 'Muscosa Rubra', which can grow up to 6½ ft. (2 m.) in height. All Moss roses thrive best in warm, dry weather.

▶ A pleasure to eye and nose alike is the fragrant, carmine-flowered Moss rose 'Henri Martin' (synonym: 'Red Moss'), whose ball-shaped flowers adorn a bush that can grow up to 5 ft. (1.5 m.) high and 6 ft. (1.8 m.) wide.

**FLOWERING:** Single; densely filled, long, globular; closed; Ø 3 in. (8 cm.); pink with dark center; intense fragrance

**GROWTH:** About 6 ft. (1.8 m.) high; strong growth, loose arches

**FEATURES:** Robust climber; exceptionally winter hardy

**PLANTING:** Beds and hedges in sunny position; also as a specimen

**INTRODUCED:** First mentioned in 1696.

# 'HERMOSA'

CHINA ROSE / Synonyms: 'Armosa', 'Mélanie Lemaire', 'Mme Neumann'

**FLOWERING:** Recurrent, with a break in fall; densely filled; Ø 2 in. (5 cm.); silver to Old rose; delicate fragrance
**GROWTH:** About 3 ft. (90 cm.) high; strong growth, arching
**FEATURES:** Protect in winter; in spring, prune as for recurrent shrub roses
**PLANTING:** Small yards and containers; very beautiful in mixed borders or in front of woody plants
**INTRODUCED:** Marcheseau, 1840, France

'Hermosa' will win you over with the old-fashioned flair of its recurrent blooms, which arch as if in a shrub. This small rose is destined for small yards or small, sunny corners of yards and patios, where in containers they will charm. If planted out in the open, they really need to be in groups of twos or threes; otherwise they will tend to lose most of their effect. There is also a climbing sport from 'Hermosa'. In 1879, Henderson introduced 'Setina' (synonym: 'Climbing Hermosa') in the United States. It has the same blooms but on long (up to 10-ft./3-m.) canes. A favorite during the Victorian age, when people were especially fond of hanging it from catenaries to form garlands, this rose is now all but forgotten.

◄ Another equally dainty China rose is the charming 'Cécile Brunner' (synonyms: 'Sweetheart Rose', 'Maltese Rose'), whose white mutation 'White Cécile Brunner' has tints of yellow and peach.

# 'OLD BLUSH'

Synonyms: *Rosa × odorata* 'Pallida', 'Parson's Pink China' / CHINA ROSE

'Old Blush' is not merely an elegant rose with very graceful flowers. Historically it is of importance as an ancestor of the Bourbons and Noisettes. Before being introduced in Europe, it had probably been cultivated in China for centuries. 'Old Blush' flowers in great clusters on slender, almost prickle-free canes. After the prime flush in June, new, cupped, pale pink flowers continue to open until winter, their petals loosely reflexed. Because of its graceful character, this rose ought to be combined with similarly refined companions in blue and gray, such as wormwood (*Artemisia*), peach-leaf bellflower (*Campanula persicifolia*), or Russian sage (*Perovskia*).

**FLOWERING:** Recurrent; half-filled, medium-sized; Ø 2½ in. (6 cm.); pale pink, darkening; sweet fragrance

**GROWTH:** 5 ft. (1.6 m.) high; upright, arching, middling strong growth

**FEATURES:** Voted World's Favorite Rose; ancient, graceful; tolerates shade and northern exposures; unfortunately, prone to fungal infection; needs protecting in winter

**PLANTING:** As a shrub rose in beds and mixed borders or as specimens; in milder regions can climb up to 8 ft. (2.5 m.)

**INTRODUCED:** Originated in China; Europe in 1789

**OTHER SYNONYMS:** 'Old Pink Monthly', 'Common Monthly', 'China Monthly', 'Monthly Rose'

# 'VIRIDIFLORA'

CHINA ROSE / Synonyms: 'Green Calyx', 'Green Rose'

**FLOWERING:** Recurrent; half-filled, small; Ø 2 in. (5 cm.); green, fringed sepals; spicy fragrance
**GROWTH:** About 2 ft. 8 in. (80 cm.) high; upright, bushy
**FEATURES:** A curiosity: lacks real blooms; robust, healthy, but needs winter protection in cold regions
**PLANTING:** A plant for rose lovers and in floral decoration
**INTRODUCED:** Mutation occurred in 1833, USA

The 'Green Rose' is a unique botanical wonder for which we can thank a petal mutation. Its fat buds open to form clusters of half-filled blooms, which, instead of typical petals, have narrow green saw-edged sepals. These are long-lasting and, as they fade, become streaked with violet and bronze. Because 'Viridiflora' lacks real flowers, it is sterile, and although it does not have the attraction of splendid, bright blooms, it does have a striking effect as a compact bedding rose or as a cut flower. With its calming green, it can prove itself as a long-lasting structural element in a mixed border. It also stands out in combinations of green and white, and green, yellow, and white.

◀ As mysterious as 'Viridiflora' is another China rose, 'Sophie's Perpetual', of whose origins nothing is known but that it was found in an old yard and reintroduced in 1960. It definitely needs protection in winter.

# 'MME ALFRED CARRIÈRE'

NOISETTE ROSE

A real treasure in the yard, 'Mme Alfred Carrière' is the star of the Noisette roses. Its seductively fragrant blooms appear in June, both singly and in clusters on long canes. Because the canes are nearly prickle free, it is almost impossible to hurt oneself on this rose, which can therefore be planted without more ado beside pillars, pergolas, arches, and seating areas. Because it grows so enthusiastically, it needs careful pruning. After flowering in July it forms laterals of almost 7 ft. (2 m.) long, and before these bud they need to be cut back to five or six eyes. Then the rose will flower sumptuously from every leaf axis until first frost. If it is not pruned, it will only flower at the tips of its laterals.

**FLOWERING:** Recurrent; loosely filled, round, cupped; large; Ø 4 in. (10 cm.); champagne with rosé tints; soon fades. Intense fragrance

**GROWTH:** 10–20 ft. (3–6 m.) high; strong-growing climber with intensive lateral growth in June; arching as bush

**FEATURES:** World's Favorite Rose; robust climber, healthy, winter hardy; tolerates half shade and sheltered northern exposure

**PLANTING:** As a large, arching bush or climber on arches, pillars, or pergolas; also in trees; not to be espaliered on south-facing walls

**INTRODUCED:** J. Schwartz, 1879, France

# 'BOULE DE NEIGE'

BOURBON ROSE

With its densely filled, white, globular flowers, the somewhat
delicate Bourbon rose 'Boule de Neige' is more than slightly
reminiscent of a snowball. When fully open, the petals on
these blooms, at first round and erect, roll up so completely
that from then on they look like heavy ball bearings. After
the first flush in June, individual blooms continue to appear
until the fall. The flowers mostly form in clusters against a
background of dark foliage, and with their purple buds have
an unusual appearance. If need be, the graceful 'Boule de
Neige' can be trained as a climber up pillars, obelisks,
and arches.

> **FLOWERING:** Recurrent; densely filled, globular; Ø 3 in. (8 cm.); white,
> often edged with dark pink; very intense fragrance
> **GROWTH:** 4 ft. (1.2 m.) high; upright, bushy, thick
> **FEATURES:** Thrives especially in half shade; needs very good soil and
> winter protection in cold areas
> **PLANTING:** Middle-sized bush suitable for planting in low hedges,
> containers, beds, and mixed borders
> **INTRODUCED:** Lacharme, 1867, France

▼ The typical globular flowers of the Bourbon rose are also
seen here on '(La) Reine Victoria', whose salmon-pink flowers
were the quintessence of the Victorian age. Unfortunately, this
5-ft. (1.5-m.) recurrent rose is also prone to black spot.

# 'SOUVENIR DE LA MALMAISON'

BOURBON ROSE / Synonym: 'Queen of Beauty and Fragrance'

**FLOWERING:** Recurrent; densely filled; large; Ø about 4 in. (11 cm.); whitish pink, fading later; Tea rose fragrance

**GROWTH:** 3 ft. (90 cm.) high, 27 in. (70 cm.) wide; delicate canes

**FEATURES:** World's Favorite Rose; optimal positioning; prone to fungal infection; suffers from damp

**PLANTING:** For small yards, beds, and containers; wonderful as cut flowers

**INTRODUCED:** Béluze, 1843, France

We advise against adding 'Souvenir de la Malmaison' to your treasury of plants in areas where it rains a good deal, because in wet weather its delicate blossoms, like those of all Bourbon roses, tend to ball and not to open again unless the outer petals are removed by hand. If not, the blooms will soon become mummified. Even in perfect weather, the weight of its billowing flowers is too much for its slender canes, and they tend to hang their heads. As if to make up for it, however, the rose has a second rich flush in the fall. Enthusiasts of this variety in milder regions can switch over to the 'Souvenir de la Malmaison' climber, a sport that can attain a height of 10 ft. (3 m.). The climber only flowers once, but its nodding flowers are seen at their best from below.

◀ The sweetest-smelling of all Bourbons has to be the recurrent 'Mme Isaac Pereire', which can reach nearly 7 ft. (2 m.). Its strong, long canes can be easily trained to climb obelisks, arches, and pergolas.

# 'GRÜSS AN TEPLITZ'

Synonyms: 'Virginia R. Coxe', 'Salut à Teplitz' / BOURBON ROSE (also classified as a CHINA ROSE)

In 1864, Rudolf Geschwind (1829–1910) published in Vienna the first book on rose breeding written in German, pleading at that early date for setting breeding objectives such as winter hardiness, healthiness, and blooming quality. He won his first laurels at the 1889 Paris Exposition Universelle with his 'Hungarian Climbing Roses', one of which is 'Grüss an Teplitz'. Today, both Geschwind and his roses have sunk into oblivion. 'Grüss an Teplitz' stands out on account of its delicate, luminous red flowers, which appear in clusters at the tips of its slender, flexible canes. If the canes are tied high up to supports, the flowers nod downward artistically. Bright blue plants such as summer sage (*Salvia nemorosa*) or larkspur (a delphinium hybrid) look wonderful as its companions.

**FLOWERING:** Recurrent; loosely filled; middle-sized; Ø 2½ in. (7 cm.); carmine with velvety dark edges, fades darker; spicy fragrance

**GROWTH:** More than 6 ft. (2 m.) high; strong, bushy, with long, flexible canes

**FEATURES:** World's Favorite Rose; requires the best soil or will be prone to mildew; winter hardy

**PLANTING:** As a shrub rose at the rear of beds; as a weeping standard; for hedges; as a climber on east-facing and west-facing walls, and on obelisks, pillars, arches, and pergolas

**INTRODUCED:** Geschwind, 1897, Austria-Hungary

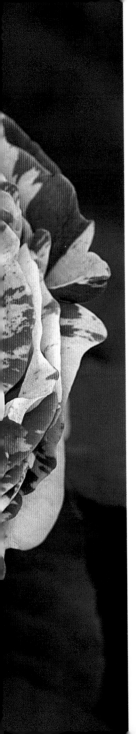

# 'VARIEGATA DI BOLOGNA'

BOURBON ROSE (also classified as a CHINA ROSE)

When in June the picturesque flowers of 'Variegata di Bologna' open in clusters, all attention should be focused on it, decked in its muted hues, for any competition would detract from its effect. Companion plants in pink, gray, or blue and violet go well with it, such as blue catmint (*Nepeta × faassenii*), which accompany the first lavish flush. Afterward, only the occasional individual flower will appear, if at all. Vita Sackville-West already discovered the hard way that 'Variegata di Bologna' thrives best in half shade (and in east-facing or west-facing positions), where its roots will be cool. Like all larger Bourbons, it also tends to spread out as a shrub if not supported.

**FLOWERING:** One-time; densely filled; quartered; at first globular, later cupped; large, Ø 3 in. (8 cm.); carmine/purple streaks and marbling on white with pink tints; bewitching fragrance
**GROWTH:** 5 ft. 4 in. (1.6 m.) high, 4 ft. (1.2 m.) wide; loose and bushy
**FEATURES:** Very attractive as a large shrub or climber; prone to fungal infection; winter hardy
**PLANTING:** As a shrub rose in beds; as a specimen; as a climber up to 12 ft. (3.5 m.)
**INTRODUCED:** Bonfiglioli, 1909, Italy

▼ By contrast, the cupped, fragrant, globular, streaked blooms of the 6-ft. (1.8-m.) high Bourbon 'Honorine de Brabant' open twice a year. With its bushy growth it is suitable as both shrub and climber.

# 'FERDINAND PICHARD'
REMONTANT ROSE

**FLOWERING:** Recurrent; filled; cupped; large; Ø 3½ in. (9 cm.); purple streaks and marbling on pinkish-white; very intense fragrance

**GROWTH:** 5 ft. (1.5 m.) high, 4 ft. (1.2 m.) wide; strong, upright, bushy

**FEATURES:** Robust, profusely flowering climber; one of the best striped roses; winter hardy

**PLANTING:** Enchanting as a specimen even in the smallest yard; also suitable in hedges, beds, and mixed borders

**INTRODUCED:** Tanne, 1921, France

As the center point of a bed or its background, 'Ferdinand Pichard' catches the eye just as much as when planted alone as a full-sized bush. Even in the smaller yard, with space enough for only one rose, this striped remontant is a good choice, as it will bloom with short breaks from June until fall. Its large, vigorous flowers usually stand in clusters just above the foliage. A sheltered planting position in full sun and regular deadheading will greatly help the blooming. In larger yards, it looks very good when planted in groups with other two-colored roses such as striped Bourbons, or with single-colored pink roses.

# 'BARON GIROD DE L'AIN'

Synonyms: 'Princess Christine von Salm', 'Royal Mondain' / REMONTANT ROSE

When planted in good soil and an ideal position, 'Baron Girod de l'Ain' will grow into a compact bush and kindle enthusiasm in June with its luxuriant, lovely clusters of flowers. In late summer, it blooms again. If conditions do not fully meet its needs in terms of light and soil, it is also happy to grow long canes that can easily be trained to climb pillars, obelisks, and arches and that can attain a height of 7–10 ft. (2–3 m.). Its velvety blossoms have the advantage of not fading in the heat and sun. This rose is exquisite among companions, whose colors will pick up its tones with dark red, white, or silver. The deep red of the flowers also makes a masterly combination with apricot and orange.

▶ At just over 3 ft. (1 m.) high, 'Roger Lambelin' also offers the play of white light reflecting from its full, fragrant blossoms. Unfortunately, this little remontant is a disappointment because of its leaves' susceptibility to fungal infection.

**FLOWERING:** Recurrent; densely filled; cupped; large; Ø 3 in. (8 cm.); carmine with chestnut tints and fine white border; purple streaks and marbling on pinkish-white; fragrant

**GROWTH:** 5 ft. (1.5 m.) high, 3 ft. (0.9 m.) wide; upright, arching, bushy, dense

**FEATURES:** Separate flowers; winter hardy

**PLANTING:** As specimens, in beds; near seating areas for its flowers and fragrance

**INTRODUCED:** Reverchon, 1897, France

# CLIMBERS

# CLIMBERS

### Classifying climbing roses
Climbing roses are the great magicians in the yard. Within just a few years they can turn the most unpromising corner of a yard into a fairy-tale scene fit for a Sleeping Beauty.

Grafted on a single stock, large-flowered climbers like 'Super Excelsa' (left) and 'Super Dorothy' (right) develop into romantic, arching, weeping standards.

Large-flowered climbers envelop shrubs, trees, walls, and pergolas with their soft, flexible canes. Usually, they flower only once, but the flush is unusually rich and lasts several weeks, the blooms often being very small but in large clusters. White is their predominant color, ahead of cool shades of pink, red, and purple. Yellow varieties hardly exist at all and, if they do, the color will be a pastel shade.

Large-flowered climbers also have fairly healthy small to medium-sized foliage that remains attractive throughout the year. In addition, they have the ability to produce long canes again and again from the base of the plant so that even if they are pruned right back (as might be done after a bitterly cold winter in which all the canes have frozen), they will be happily blooming again within three years.

With their thick, strong canes, climbers (or climbing roses in the strict sense) are branching scramblers. They can grow 7 ft. (2 m.) and more vertically, using their thorns to hold themselves up. They also have fairly large flowers, either single blossoms or in clusters, and usually flower more than once a year. Climbers also come in yellow, scarlet, orange, salmon pink, and apricot, colors that are virtually nonexistent among large-flowered climbers.

**PAGES 58–9**
The large-flowered climber 'Alexandre Girault' envelops the summer-house and arched walkway of the Roseraie du Val-de-Marne with fragrant majesty. One of the most impressive rose gardens in the world, the Roseraie was created in 1898 in l'Haÿ, and first went by the name Roseraie de l'Haÿ-les-Roses.

**ROSES ON OBELISKS, PYRAMIDS, AND PILLARS**
When planting roses by obelisks and pyramids, it is usual to plant a single plant in the middle of the support frame; while when planting roses beside larger pillars, it is usual to plant two opposite each other. In both cases the canes can be trained to grow in a upward spiral and if possible flush against the support frame. Cutting main canes back early encourages growth.

The blossoms of 'New Dawn' bring their tender magic to the tall windows of this house. To adorn such narrow architectural elements, you should use only pillar roses or climbers, whose growth is limited.

## Pruning once-flowering climbing roses

Once-flowering climbers and large-flowered climbers that are growing over walls or up trees do not need pruning even after they flower. Many go on subsequently to produce a wealth of hips. If on the other hand they are being espaliered, or grown up pergolas or arches and need to retain their shape, roses that have already developed a framework should be given their main pruning in July or August, after they have flowered. This involves removing laterals that have flowered back to the point on the primary from which they are growing. It is important to leave the branch collar intact so that the buds that are dormant in it can form new shoots and replace the twigs that are removed. When it comes to roses with only a few main canes, cut the laterals back to only two or three eyes. Since the current year's new growth will be next year's flowering canes, they should be left untouched.

## Pruning recurrent climbing roses

The time to prune recurrent climbers is in March. Most climbers flower on the current year's laterals on canes that are from one to several years old. To prevent plant senility, it is always advisable for the framework of the plant to be made up of canes of different ages, from the ground up.

For older roses with many canes, one or two primary canes should be removed each year, if possible from the base. Long canes from the previous year should remain untouched if they are destined to form part of the framework. Strong laterals from these primary canes should be pruned back to two or three eyes; weak ones are best cut right back to the point on the primary from which they are growing. During early spring pruning, all frozen, dead, or broken canes should of course be removed as well.

# 'SYMPATHIE®'
CLIMBER / Synonym: 'Sympathy'

**FLOWERING:** Recurrent;
filled; cupped; large;
Ø 4 in. (10 cm.); dark,
velvety red; fragrant
**GROWTH:** Strong,
10–13 ft. (3–4 m.) high;
lots of twigs and branches
**FEATURES:** ADR Rose 1966;
robust climbing rose; rain
resistant; very winter hardy
**PLANTING:** For pergolas,
pillars, summer-houses,
walls, arches
**INTRODUCED:** Kordes, 1964,
Germany

When it comes to planting climbing roses to cover walls
or vertical spaces, 'Sympathie®' is one of the favorite
choices, for the unusual effect not only of its velvety deep
red, which glows without being gaudy, but also of the
blossoms themselves, reminiscent of hybrid Teas, that
appear individually or in clusters from June through fall.
Because over time this robust variety produces thick,
woody, branching canes that blossom at their top while their
base remains bare, it is advisable to cut back hard in the
lower third of the plant in order to prompt yearlings to grow
and branch out. Alternatively, plant tall grasses or bushes in
front, or a thickly flowering clematis to climb together with
the rose.

◄ If you are planting a rose to embellish your house, never
plant it on a south-facing wall. It won't like the heat. The
once-flowering climber 'Paul's Scarlet Climber' is almost
tailor-made for half shade or cold spots. Its half-filled,
flame-red blooms will cover pillars, walls, and pergolas up
to a height of 13 ft. (4 m.).

# 'DORTMUND®'
## CLIMBER

'Dortmund®' is undemanding and reliable. Even in half shade and in poorer soil its splendid great clusters of blood-red blossoms will create a feel of burgeoning vitality, especially because of the white eyes in the midst of the great blossoms that leave a cheerful, unpretentious impression, which is why the variety is so suited to out of town and country gardens. Whether adorning a shed, or adding color to a fence or arch, it will always attract the eye. In larger country gardens, 'Dortmund®' can be left on its own to grow without any support or as an imposing specimen. As soon as it starts to produce hips, it is advisable to remove them from the late flowering.

**FLOWERING:** Recurrent; single; large; Ø 4 in. (10 cm.); blood-red with white eye; delicate fragrance

**GROWTH:** Strong; 10 ft. (3 m.) high; long, multiple canes

**FEATURES:** ADR Rose 1954; robust, healthy climbing rose; tolerates heat and half shade; rain resistant; produces hips; very winter hardy

**PLANTING:** For pergolas, pillars, arbors, bowers, summer-houses, walls, arches; also as specimens

**INTRODUCED:** Kordes, 1955, Germany

# 'FLAMMENTANZ®'

CLIMBER / Synonym: 'Flame Dance'

Its extravagant, brilliant red display is the way 'Flammentanz®' apologizes for blooming only once. The long-lasting, colorful effect of this climber is the result not only of its small and medium-sized blood-red flowers but also of the fact that they always bloom in clusters. The spectacle begins in June, continuing for six weeks. On top of that, the variety is also rain resistant and its colors only start to fade shortly before withering. In the fall, it catches the eye once more with a profusion of both oval and globular hips as large as ¾ in. (2 cm.) across. These merely add to the rose's already high decorative value.

**FLOWERING:** One-time; loosely filled; large; Ø 3½ in. (9 cm.); blood-red; little scent
**GROWTH:** 10–16 ft. (3–5 m.); strong, stiff, thick
**FEATURES:** ADR Quality Certificate 1952; robust, profusely flowering climber; suits half shade; tolerates southerly exposures, but not by house walls; the frost-hardiest red climber
**PLANTING:** For espaliering, pergolas, pillars, arbors, bowers, summer-houses, walls, arches; also hanging from walls
**INTRODUCED:** Kordes, 1955, Germany

# 'ROSARIUM UETERSEN®'

CLIMBER / Synonyms: 'Kordes' Rose Rosarium Uetersen', 'Seminole Wind', 'Utersen'

**FLOWERING:** Recurrent; densely filled, large; Ø 4½ in. (12 cm.); warm pinkish red, fading later to silvery tints; subtle apple scent

**GROWTH:** 7–10 ft. (2–3 m.) high; upright, thick, branching to bushy; strong, stiff, thick

**FEATURES:** Robust, profusely flowering climber; suits northerly exposure; tolerates southerly exposures, but not by house walls; very winter hardy

**PLANTING:** For pillars, obelisks, lower walls; as a solid shrub rose by a fence or as a specimen used as a space divider; a fabulous weeping standard

**INTRODUCED:** Kordes, 1977, Germany

Anyone who has ever had this rose—with its very special, warm, strong pink tints—in their yard will recognize it instantly, its old-fashioned expressiveness. When this climber's flowers open in clusters in June, a play of color begins that will last right until the flowers start to fade and take on a silvery sheen, at the same time as the bush itself continues tirelessly sending out fresh pink blossoms. This variety is a source of fascination until first frost; even in small yards it should not be missed, where it can be planted by an obelisk in a bed or by an arch next to a yard path. But it is as a long-stemmed rose that its charm is most delightful. Grafted at about 4½ ft. (1.4 m.) up on another stem, it grows into a little tree with a very picturesque round crown.

# 'ETUDE'
Synonym: 'Étude' / CLIMBER

The bright pink, slightly reflexed, half-filled blossoms of 'Etude' make a sumptuous display. After the main flowering in June and July, the clusters on this climber do not come to an abrupt halt but rather rebloom in late summer in another rich show of color. A gentle break can be provided to these thrilling spectacles by combining them with clematis hybrids such as 'Nelly Moser', 'Bees Jubilee', 'Capitaine Thuilleaux', or 'Carnaby', which, like the rose, blossom in June and again in late summer, and whose star-shaped, pale and dark striped flowers set off its intense color.

Even though 'Etude' can tolerate a southerly exposure if it has good air circulation, neither it nor the clematis hybrids should be planted where they will be exposed to the midday sun without being protected.

▶ Obelisks, pillars, fences, and arches look wonderful when enfolded in the full, dark pink to cherry-red blossoms of the healthy recurrent climber 'Parade'. Their color and fragrance are slightly reminiscent of Old roses.

**FLOWERING:** Recurrent; half filled; Ø 3 in. (8 cm.); dark pinkish-red; fragrant
**GROWTH:** 10 ft. (3 m.) high
**FEATURES:** Robust, profusely flowering climber; suits northerly exposures; tolerates southerly exposures, but not by house walls; winter hardy
**PLANTING:** For pillars, obelisks, arches, and walls; as a shrub rose to hang over a fence or as a space divider in the yard
**INTRODUCED:** Gregory, 1965, Great Britain

# 'MME GRÉGOIRE STAECHELIN'

CLIMBER / Synonym: 'Spanish Beauty'

'Mme Grégoire Staechelin' flowers from the beginning of June and, as can be seen, makes a delicate and charming pair when planted with irises. Its flowers, with their wonderful fragrance, appear only once a year, but in breathtaking profusion. In the fall, the flowers are followed by large, pear-shaped, orange hips. With its slightly withered, hanging blooms, this vigorous rose reminds one of the olden days and looks best when seen from below and when its scent can be enjoyed from close at hand. It is at its most advantageous when growing against a bright easterly or westerly wall or pergola. If one wishes, it can be combined with a late-summer blooming variety of *Clematis-viticella* or kiwi vine (*Actinidia kolomikta*), which has tendrils that will twist into the rose.

**FLOWERING:** One-time bloomer; half filled, hanging; large; Ø 4 in. (10 cm.); light pink with darker underside; breathtaking fragrance
**GROWTH:** 13 ft. (4 m.) high; strong; upright; bushy
**FEATURES:** Picturesque, profusely flowering; produces a wealth of large, orange hips; suits northerly exposures too, but needs winter protection
**PLANTING:** Enchanting on bright walls, pillars, obelisks, pergolas, and arches; for pillars, obelisks, arches, and walls; as a shrub rose to hang over a fence or as a space divider in the yard
**INTRODUCED:** Dot, 1927, Spain

# 'CONSTANCE SPRY®'
CLIMBER

**FLOWERING:** One-time
bloomer; densely filled,
cupped; large; Ø 4½ in.
(11 cm.); pink; strong
fragrance

**GROWTH:** 13 ft. (4 m.) high;
strong, arching, thick

**FEATURES:** Modern romantic
rose; the first English rose;
suits walls in half shade
and northerly exposures;
very winter hardy

**PLANTING:** For pillars,
obelisks, pergolas, house
and yard walls; against
a fence or as a strong
shrub rose; wonderful as a
weeping standard

**INTRODUCED:** Austin, 1961,
Great Britain

'Constance Spry®' was the first rose grown by David
Austin, to which many, many subsequent English roses
trace back their ancestry. Although it grows in somewhat
unruly fashion and flowers only once, the flowers
themselves are large and as lovely as a dream, opening
into deep cups from little round balls. It can be grown as
a strong, slightly disorderly, arching bush of up to about
7 ft. (2 m.) high, or even as an impenetrable, thorny
hedge. It is much more charming, however, as a climbing
rose over a support, which will give its canes something to
hold on to. Then it will clamber over a 13-ft. (4-m.) wall,
or grace a pergola, tripod, or fence. From the end of June
until August, its pink blossoms with their silver-tinted
outer edges will bathe a yard in the magic of a fairy tale.

# 'COMPASSION®'

Synonym: 'Belle de Londres' / CLIMBER

'Compassion®' has been part of the standard repertoire of climbers for years. Although what won over gardeners' hearts at first was the Tea-rose shape of its flowers (at that time its color was not exactly fashionable), now the situation has reversed completely: soft apricot and salmon pink are all the rage. And here the rose, with its good continuity, has something special to offer: a bloom with enchanting changeability. Although nowadays people are a bit taken aback by the almost too perfectly turned shape of its flowers, everyone is mad about Old roses and their dense, bushy forms, as evidenced by the English roses and the romantic old-fashioned roses. Ultimately, one has to concede that 'Compassion®' does some things right: it blooms in beautiful clusters and has a fragrance that is simply enchanting.

**FLOWERING:** Recurrent; loosely filled, like hybrid Teas; large; Ø 5 in. (12 cm.); salmon pink with apricot tints; intense fragrance

**GROWTH:** 7–10 ft (2–3 m.) high; upright, stiff canes, bushes out

**FEATURES:** ADR Quality Certificate 1976; robust, profusely flowering climber; winter hardy

**PLANTING:** For pillars, obelisks, low walls; can be espaliered; as a strong shrub rose against a fence, as a specimen or hedge

**INTRODUCED:** Harkness, 1972, Great Britain

# 'GLOIRE DE DIJON'

HISTORIC CLIMBER / Synonyms: 'Old Glory', 'Glory John'

**FLOWERING:** Recurrent; densely filled; large; Ø 4 in. (10 cm.); pale orange-yellow, creamy-white edges, with pink tints; fragrant

**GROWTH:** Up to 16 ft. (5 m.) high; upright and strong

**FEATURES:** Needs optimal planting position; prone to black spot; not rain resistant and needs winter protection

**PLANTING:** For pillars, obelisks, yard walls, pergolas; can be espaliered; wonderful as a weeping standard

**INTRODUCED:** Jacotot, 1853, France

'Gloire de Dijon' is one of the most beautiful and expressive of all the historic climbing roses. Its lovely blooms often open from dark yellow buds by the end of May and then go on, depending on the trace minerals present in the soil, to assume the color of cognac, with yellow and pink tints. And it goes on flowering until first frost. Anyone who has ever had 'Gloire de Dijon' in their yard has relished its reliability—and rued its weaknesses, too: its susceptibility to black spot and the habit its blooms have of balling in rainy weather. Its blooms make a wonderful contrast with the violet of the butterfly bush (*Buddleia alternifolia*) or blue and violet clematis. Its seductive charm is also evident when growing against an obelisk in a bed of white and yellow.

# 'GOLDEN SHOWERS®'
## CLIMBER

The bright yellow blooms of 'Golden Showers®' open singly or in clusters from June and continue until first frost, with an endless variety of highlights. Because the flowers fade as they age, their colors have many different shades and tonalities. When this rose is planted as a shrub toward the back of a border, or as a standard or climber against an obelisk or pyramid in the middle of a bed, the color-play of its blooms harmonizes wonderfully against a setting of white, yellow, and blue, or among yellow, orange, and scarlet, with silver and gray leaves as a contrast. To keep the rose healthy and blossoming well, it needs to be given a good, balanced rose feed.

▶ Of a similar color but resistant to rain is 'Goldener Olymp®', a robust, very winter-hardy rose with a delightful scent to its blooms. Its canes can extend to a length of over 8 ft. (2.5 m.), which makes it suitable for planting as either a climber or a shrub.

**FLOWERING:** Recurrent; loosely filled, flattening; large; Ø 4½ in. (11 cm.); yellow, turning to light yellow; light scent

**GROWTH:** 7–10 ft. (2–3 m.) high; strong, upright, bushy, thick

**FEATURES:** Robust and profusely flowering; half shade; winter hardy

**PLANTING:** For pillars, obelisks, arches; can be espaliered; also a shrub rose and a specimen

**INTRODUCED:** Lammerts, 1956, USA

# 'ELFE IV®'
CLIMBER

**FLOWERING:** Recurrent; densely filled, quartered; large; Ø 4½ in. (12 cm.); greenish creamy yellow; light scent

**GROWTH:** 8–10 ft. (2.5–3 m.) high; upright, bushy

**FEATURES:** Modern rose, old-fashioned climber; needs warm, sunny, sheltered planting position; winter hardy

**PLANTING:** For pillars, obelisks, pyramids, house walls, pergolas; can be espaliered; also wonderful as a specimen

**INTRODUCED:** Tantau, 2000, Germany

When in June the unusual blooms of the old-fashioned climbing rose 'Elfe IV®' start to appear, it is hard to see enough of them, for they are so reminiscent of the densely filled blossoms of the Old roses. Unfortunately, like so many Old roses, they also suffer from the wet, and like so many white and pastel-colored flowers, are liable to red spotting, turning brown, and balling. None of this, however, should take away from the beauty of this rose, for it continues to bloom and in the fall has a second flush to charm us with—provided, of course, that this warmth-loving sun-worshiper is planted in a sheltered position with good air circulation and lots of sun; and provided, too, of course, that this does not happen to be against a south-facing house wall, for the dry air and heat that accumulate there will inevitably damage any rose.

# 'ILSE KROHN SUPERIOR®'
CLIMBER

With its blossoms like those of white hybrid Teas glowing singly or in small clusters above its dark foliage, 'Ilse Krohn Superior®' is still a classic among white climbing roses. This lovely rose can also be grown in large containers or as a picturesque specimen on its slender stem, towering over flower or vegetable beds. Its profuse flush starts in June and continues pleasingly thereafter. If you share the emerging predilection for old-fashioned rose shapes, you will be rather more interested in the new white climbers such as 'Uetersener Klosterrose' (Tantau, 2006) or 'Graciosa' (Noack, 2002), with their romantic flair. Regardless of the shape of their blooms, however, all white climbers are enchanting when twilight comes and they start to glow, as if by magic.

▶ 'Direktor Benschop' (synonyms: 'Direktor Benshop', 'City of York'), a shrub that grows up to 15 ft. (4.5 m.) tall, is known for its half-filled, creamy-white blooms. Although they appear only once a year, they make up for it with the exuberance of their long-lasting flush.

**FLOWERING:** Recurrent; densely filled, like hybrid Tea; large; Ø 4 in. (10 cm.); white; heavy scent
**GROWTH:** 10 ft. (3 m.) high; upright, with long arching canes; strong, bushy
**FEATURES:** Thrives in half shade; healthy, winter hardy
**PLANTING:** For pillars, obelisks, pyramids, house walls, pergolas; can be espaliered; also wonderful as a specimen; petals well suited to use in rose recipes
**INTRODUCED:** Kordes, 1964, Germany

# 'BOBBIE JAMES'

LARGE-FLOWERED CLIMBER / Synonym: 'Bobby James'

**FLOWERING:** One-time bloomer; loosely half-filled; Ø 2 in. (5 cm.); creamy white; sweet fragrance

**GROWTH:** Up to 30 ft. (9 m.) high; extremely vigorous

**FEATURES:** Thrives in half shade; in colder regions, its lower half needs winter protection; dark-red, oval hips

**PLANTING:** Only for trees and large surfaces

**INTRODUCED:** Sunningdale Nurseries, 1961, Great Britain

'Bobbie James' is an example of a splendid, energetic rose that deserves careful thought before being planted in the yard. When it wraps a pillar, pergola, or tree in its dense, white garlands, it puts on a highly artistic show of romantic spontaneity. But for it to achieve this effect, its support must be very stable indeed: trees that are still young and growing or just graceful in their own right, or pillars and pergolas made of slender poles, simply won't be up to the task. As time goes by, this rose just puts on more and more weight, and is heavier still in winter when wet snow weighs down its thick canes. The weight of a nine-year-old 'Bobbie James' in winter is once said to have bent a solid aluminum pole in two and crushed it.

◀ A climber that grows energetically up to 30 ft. (9 m.) and as loosely as 'Bobbie James' is 'Wedding Day', a pure-white one-time bloomer. In the fall it outdoes itself with an excellent, decorative display of small, red hips.

# 'SEAGULL'
## LARGE-FLOWERED CLIMBER

When in July the large-flowered climber 'Seagull' drapes the yard with its flowery white veil, it suffuses it at the same time with its sweet scent, calling the bees to a feast. This one-time bloomer can climb trees well over 23 ft. (7 m.) high with ease. Its strong growth is accompanied by a flush just as rich—pure white blossoms with luxurious yellow stamens opening from lemon yellow buds. 'Seagull' blossoms in such huge, often round clusters that it almost covers the gray-green foliage below. An unforgettable sight! It fits happily into the most informal, even semi-wild garden, where it can clamber up trees and bushes, but it does so too in a formal one, where it will, of course, need pillars, pergolas, or arches—not to mention a determined hand—to maintain its shape.

▶ Anything 'Seagull' can do, 'Sander's White Rambler' (synonym: 'Sanders White') can do too…but on a smaller scale. At a mere 11½ ft. (3.5 m.) high, this one-time bloomer is eminently suited to small yards, low trees, rose arches, pergolas, and pillars.

**FLOWERING:** One-time bloomer; half-filled; Ø 1½ in. (4 cm.); white; very intense fragrance

**GROWTH:** 13–20 ft. (4–6 m.) high; strong, many canes

**FEATURES:** Tolerates half shade; small, orange hips; relatively winter hardy

**PLANTING:** For yard walls and freestanding climbing supports; climbs in trees and shrubs and over hedges

**INTRODUCED:** Pritchard, 1907, Great Britain

# 'RAMBLING RECTOR'

LARGE-FLOWERED CLIMBER

'Rambling Rector' is a one-time bloomer
that grows up to 23 ft. (7 m.) high. The
unrestrained growth of this large-flowered
climber is accompanied by a flush of equally
uninhibited profusion. Its great clusters
of small white blossoms recall nothing so
much as whirls of whipped cream, and are
an unforgettable sight, especially against
their gray-green foliage, a vision of delight
matched only by the waves of fruity, sweet
fragrance they exude. 'Rambling Rector'
is ideal as a precious, fragrant addition to a
pillar or arbor, to arches over benches, or a
seating area located under trees up which it
rambles. A tip: if it is grown to climb a single
tree, as shown here, when it is fully grown
why not plant a slow-growing ivy at its base
to cover that unsightly bareness?

**FLOWERING:** One-time bloomer; loosely half-filled;
small; Ø 1½ in. (4 cm.); white with yellow stamens;
intense fragrance

**GROWTH:** 16–23 ft. (5–7 m.) high; strong, bushy

**FEATURES:** Profuse, exuberant flush; suits northerly
exposures, half shade and light woodland; produces
an abundance of small hips in late summer;
winter hardy

**PLANTING:** Robust climber; clambers up trees and over
hedges; glorious when espaliered and on pergolas,
pillars, and arbors

**INTRODUCED:** Unknown; in Great Britain before 1910

# 'ADÉLAÏDE D'ORLÉANS'
LARGE-FLOWERED CLIMBER

**FLOWERING:** One-time
  bloomer; loosely half-
  filled; medium-sized;
  Ø 2 in. (5 cm.); creamy
  white with pink tints;
  sweet fragrance
**GROWTH:** 13–16 ft (4–5 m.)
  high; strong, with long,
  soft canes; bushy
**FEATURES:** Elegant, foaming
  flush; suits northern
  exposures and half shade;
  usually evergreen;
  winter hardy
**PLANTING:** Exquisite on large
  rose arches, colonnades,
  pergolas, and pillars; a tree
  climber
**INTRODUCED:** Jacques, 1826,
  France

With the delicate nuances of its coloration and the silky-edged petals that lie like small lace ruffs around the stamens at the center of its blooms, 'Adélaïde d'Orléans' is every inch a genuine Old rose. Its delicately crumpled blooms usually first appear in great, thick clusters in July and, together with its pink buds, make a simply enchanting sight. With its elegant appearance, this large-flowered climber looks splendid on pillars, arches (as above, at Mottisfont), and pergolas, but it can also be grown over trees and bushes. It was much loved in Victorian times, when with other *Rosa sempervirens* sports, such as 'Félicité et Perpétue', it was not unjustifiably regarded as an "evergreen rose."

# 'VENUSTA PENDULA'
LARGE-FLOWERED CLIMBER

Straddling this single-beamed pergola, 'Venusta Pendula' reaches through the yard in a single flood of mother-of-pearl colored blossoms. What a delightful idea, to find a place for such a vigorously growing rose in such a small yard, where it fills a variety of roles: not just as a way of dividing the area or of adding an element of height to provide spaciousness, but also as a romantic feature, with its blossoms forming a frame through which the house and yard can be seen in an endless variety of views. The choice of a single-beam pergola has the further advantage of leaving only a little of the ground in shadow, so that lawns and flowerbeds can be placed beside it. To achieve that picturesque look, the flexible canes of 'Venusta Pendula' are easy to lay over a yard wall or string in garlands along a catenary.

▶ The charming, full, fragrant little blooms of 'Paul's Himalayan Musk Rambler' also change from pale pink to white. Growing to a height of over 30 ft. (10 m.), this one-time blooming giant can cause old trees to sway.

**FLOWERING:** One-time bloomer; loosely half-filled; small; Ø 1½ in. (4 cm.); pale pink, fading to white

**GROWTH:** 20 ft. (6 m.) high; very strong

**FEATURES:** Northern exposures and half shade; single, globular hips; winter hardy

**PLANTING:** A tree climber; suitable for espaliering, and for pillars and pergolas; also beside water and in light woodland gardens

**INTRODUCED:** Old variety, reintroduced 1928 by Kordes, Germany

# 'MAY QUEEN I'
LARGE-FLOWERED CLIMBER

**FLOWERING:** One-time
bloomer; loosely half filled;
medium-sized; Ø 2½ in.
(6 cm.); pale pink with
violet tints; sweet fragrance
**GROWTH:** 10–13 ft. (3–4 m.)
high; strong, bushy, long
canes
**FEATURES:** Robust, luxuriant
flowers; northern exposures,
and half shade; winter hardy
**PLANTING:** A tree climber;
exquisite when espaliered
and on pillars and pergolas,
and as a weeping standard
**INTRODUCED:** Manda, 1898,
USA

Not all large-flowered climbers have small, clustered
blooms; some, indeed, have flowers so large they remind
one of climbers. These belong to a group, all of which
date back to the turn of the 20th century, which was
developed by crossing *Rosa wichuraiana* with large-
blossomed hybrids. In this the primary breeders were
Barbier in France and Manda in the United States. 'May
Queen I' was the first of the Manda varieties and was
named for its early blossoming. With its flexible canes
and gently hanging blooms, this lovely rose is especially
charming when grown on pergolas and pillars near seating
areas, where the beauty and fragrance of its flowers can be
enjoyed at eye level and from close by.

◄ Showers of great, loosely filled pink flowers also
mark the flush in June and July of 'Johanna Röpke'.
Surprisingly, this robust, impressive large-flowered
climber, which grows to a height of 13 ft. (4 m.), has
somewhat fallen into oblivion.

# 'NEW DAWN'
## LARGE-FLOWERED CLIMBER

'New Dawn' is a star among climbing roses, but without the allure of a diva. Against the thick, dark gleam of its foliage, its breath-soft, pearly pink flowers, not unlike those of a hybrid Tea in size and shape, cast an unbroken spell from June until fall, proving their worth against house and yard walls (provided they are not facing due south) and on arches, pergolas, pillars, and obelisks. This long-lasting, pale pink flush not only makes for a romantic yard but also harmonizes astonishingly well with flowers of every other color, producing ethereal impressions when combined with a light blue clematis such as 'Blue Angel' or a pale pink one such as 'Nelly Moser'.

**FLOWERING:** Recurrent; loosely filled; large; Ø 3½ in. (9 cm.); porcelain pink; fragrant

**GROWTH:** 10–13 ft. (3–4 m.) high; strong, bushy

**FEATURES:** Superb climber with long, thick foliage; rain resistant; tolerates heat; also for growing in half shade and containers; very winter hardy

**PLANTING:** Yard walls and freestanding supports, and as a weeping standard

**INTRODUCED:** Somerset Nursery, 1930, USA

▶ Even larger, fuller, pale pink flowers can be found on 'Mme de Sancy de Parabère', an historic Boursault rose. This 13-ft. (4-m.) climber, which scrambles up on prickle-free canes, blossoms only once, but how extravagantly, and with such seductive fragrance.

# 'DÉBUTANTE I'
LARGE-FLOWERED CLIMBER / Synonym: 'Mother's Day Rose'

**FLOWERING:** One-time
bloomer; densely filled;
medium-sized; Ø 2 in.
(5 cm.); pink; sweet
fragrance

**GROWTH:** 10 ft. (3 m.) high,
6½ ft. (2 m.) wide; strong,
bushy, branching

**FEATURES:** Comes into bloom
in July; suits half shade;
produces a wealth of small
hips in late summer;
winter hardy

**PLANTING:** A tree climber;
exquisite when espaliered
and when grown on
pergolas, obelisks, and
pyramids; wonderful as a
standard

**INTRODUCED:** Walsh, 1902,
USA

For reasons of space alone, this sort of rosy medley
created by interlacing arches is really only possible in
a park-like yard. Yet when planning a rose garden one
should not give up at the start, because climbers can
offer impressive solutions even in smaller yards. The
two climbers growing against this pillar in the gardens
of Mottisfont Abbey, the pink 'Débutante I' and the
deep purple 'Bleu Magenta', demonstrate the variety
of different flowering patterns that obtains among
ramblers. While the somewhat larger single blooms
of 'Débutante I' create something of an airy, fanciful
impression, the densely filled, dark flush of 'Bleu
Magenta' comes in thick, giant clusters. The combination
is also masterful because both varieties, although one-time
flowerers, come into bloom at the same time, in July.

# 'MARIA LISA'

Synonyms: 'Maria Liesa', 'Maria Lise' / LARGE-FLOWERED CLIMBER

With its closely bunched clusters of little, wild-rose blooms, 'Maria Lisa' brings to mind a pink version of *Rosa multiflora*, which is, in fact, one of its ancestors. In June and July its hard-wearing little flowers open, filling the yard with liveliness and gaiety, an effect that is underlined wonderfully well by white, purple, and deep red roses and shrubs as well as violet clematis. 'Maria Lisa' has also proved its worth on pillars, colonnades, and arches over paths—or near seating areas, where its prickle-free canes can neither hurt nor impede anyone. In late summer, it produces yet another color accent in the shape of small, red hips that uncannily resemble a weeping standard.

▶ Set in small, half-filled, fragrant blossoms, whose colors vary from carmine to lilac and grayish violet, the white eyes of 'Veilchenblau' (synonyms: 'Blue Rambler', 'Blue Rosalie', 'Violet Blue') peep at the sun from the top of its long, 15-ft. (4.5-m.), prickle-free canes.

**FLOWERING:** One-time bloomer; single; small; Ø under 1 in. (2 cm.); pink with white eye; sweet fragrance
**GROWTH:** 7–10 ft. (2–3 m.) high; strong, prickle-free canes
**FEATURES:** Suits half shade; small hips; not in cold areas or planting positions
**PLANTING:** Good on arches, pillars, pergolas, obelisks, and pyramids; also trees; not by sunny house walls
**INTRODUCED:** Liebau, 1925, Germany

# 'SUPER EXCELSA', 'SUPER DOROTHY'
LARGE-FLOWERED CLIMBER

**FLOWERING:** Recurrent; densely filled; small; Ø under 1½ in. (3 cm.); luminous carmine
**GROWTH:** 7–10 ft. (2–3 m.) high; thin, soft canes; bushy
**FEATURES:** ADR Quality Certificate 1991. Winter hardy
**PLANTING:** Suitable for espaliering and pegging down, on obelisks, pillars, and arches, and against fences; glorious as a weeping standard
**INTRODUCED:** Hetzel, 1986, Germany

In 1986, 'Super Excelsa' with its cool carmine (left) and 'Super Dorothy' with its warmer red (right) came on the market. Apart from their difference in color, these two delightful large-flowered climbers have exactly the same characteristics, both being stronger derivatives of the world famous but, alas, mildew-prone varieties 'Dorothy Perkins' and 'Excelsa' (synonym: 'Red Dorothy Perkins'). 'Super Excelsa' and 'Super Dorothy' often start to bloom only in July, but so exuberantly that the fresh colors of their blossoms catch every eye. As weeping standards they almost trail their flowering canes on the ground, and as climbing roses are worth thinking about for small yard accents such as pillars, arches, or obelisks. They also look very artistic as bushes, leaning against a fence.

◀ Another of the most tried-and-tested large-flowered climbers is 'Chevy Chase', with its clusters of densely filled, fragrant little flowers that burst into flame in July. This strongly colored climber can swing up to a height of nearly 20 ft. (6 m.).

# 'RUSSELIANA'

Synonyms: 'Old Spanish Rose', 'Russell's Cottage Rose' / LARGE-FLOWERED CLIMBER

No matter how lovely it may seem, when a site is set aside for a climbing rose between the wall of the house and the patio, not every variety is suitable, especially when the patio faces south and radiates hot air. Like the hybrid multifloras, 'Russeliana' does not thrive against south-facing walls. On the other hand, this large-flowered climber comes into its full glory in an easterly or westerly position with good air circulation, especially when it stands close to the similarly colored flowers and silver leaves of Rose Campion (*Lychnis coronaria*), as seen here. With its somewhat rustic charm, this rose fits in well as a bush in country or large, semi-wild gardens, either as an onlooker or as a weeping standard. Either way, the nuances of the colors of its blossoms will provide endless fascination.

**FLOWERING:** One-time bloomer; filled; flat; medium-sized; Ø 2 in. (5 cm.); purple, fading later; lovely fragrance

**GROWTH:** Up to 20 ft. (6 m.) high; strong, bushy

**FEATURES:** Robust climbing rose; resistant to disease; suitable for northerly exposures and half shade; very winter hardy

**PLANTING:** A tree climber; breathtaking on pergolas and pillars, and as an arching shrub

**INTRODUCED:** Probably circa 1840, Spain

**OTHER SYNONYMS:** 'Scarlet Grevillei', 'Souvenir de la Bataille de Marengo'

# 'ALBÉRIC BARBIER'
LARGE-FLOWERED CLIMBER

With apparently artless country charm, 'Albéric Barbier' graces this bird house; but the fact that the yellow of the wall and the creamy yellow of the eye of the rose are identical gives the game away. Yes: this variety was chosen with a very careful eye for design. If you are looking for a climbing rose to adorn the wall of your house or garden wall, you will achieve a truly artistic effect if the tint of the rose and the color of the wall match closely. Here, the fragrant large-flowered climber 'Albéric Barbier', which reblooms in late summer, offers the viewer an endlessly changing play of colors and shapes that seems almost alive. As its hybrid Tea-like blossoms fade from yellowish to creamy white, they become star-shaped as the outer petals reflex and roll up.

**FLOWERING:** Remontant; densely filled; large; Ø 3 in. (8 cm.); yellowish at first, then creamy white with yellowish tints at its center; lovely fragrance

**GROWTH:** Up to 16 ft. (5 m.) high; very strong, bushy, long, flexible, widely spreading canes

**FEATURES:** Robust, romantic climbing rose; suitable for northerly exposures and half shade; winter hardy

**PLANTING:** A tree climber; breath-taking on pergolas, arches, and pillars; magical as a weeping standard; can also be planted on banks as ground cover

**INTRODUCED:** Barbier, 1900, France

▼ With its large, romantic blossoms, 'Alchymist' is another charming rose. This 13-ft. (4-m.) one-time bloomer produces densely filled, fragrant, apricot and pink rosettes that give it the flair of an Old rose.

# 'GOLDFINCH'
## LARGE-FLOWERED CLIMBER

**FLOWERING:** One-time
bloomer; half filled; flat;
medium-sized; Ø 2½ in.
(6 cm.); apricot yellow at
first, then fading to creamy
white; delicate fragrance

**GROWTH:** Up to 10 ft. (3 m.)
high; bushy, with long,
flexible canes

**FEATURES:** Robust climbing
rose with almost prickle-
free canes; produces
globular hips in late
summer; very winter hardy

**PLANTING:** Ideal for small
yards; climbs small
woody plants; exquisite
on pergolas and pillars
or as an arching shrub;
picturesque as a weeping
standard

**INTRODUCED:** W. Paul, 1907,
Great Britain

'Goldfinch', with its luxuriant single flush, is one of the
few yellow large-flowered climbers. It has umbels of
primrose-yellow blossoms opening in June and July from
apricot-colored buds, which then lighten to creamy white,
with a sweet scent like that of the cowslip. The newly
open rosettes form striking clusters of yellow stamens,
which will darken to black as time passes. In this way,
'Goldfinch' puts on an ever-changing display of shades of
yellow and white throughout its period of blossoming. In
direct sunlight, because the flowers very quickly fade to
white, the show is far less lively; it is at its loveliest in half
shade or light shade.

# 'GHISLAINE DE FÉLIGONDE'

### LARGE-FLOWERED CLIMBER

'Ghislaine de Féligonde' does not stand apart from the pattern of other large-flowered climbers just because of its yellow color, but also because it is recurrent and far less inclined than most of the others to reach up to the very heavens. Its graceful growth and ability, after its first flush in June and July, to rebloom splendidly in late summer make it a pièce de résistance for the small yard. All of which makes it even the more surprising that for all its charm and enchanting beauty, this rose is still very little known. Of course, it is essential to remember to take the secateurs and deadhead the rose after its first flowers have faded, otherwise the rebloom will be weak. 'Ghislaine de Féligonde' is particularly enchanting when planted as a weeping standard beside a path or seating area, or on its slender stem in a bed towering over other flowers.

▶ The densely filled blossoms of 'Madeleine Seltzer' (synonym: 'Yellow Tausendschön'), a one-time bloomer that grows to 10 ft. (3 m.) tall, offer the same play of color as 'Ghislaine de Féligonde', from yellow to white, except here in a bright lemon yellow.

**FLOWERING:** Remontant; loosely filled; flat; small; Ø 2 in. (5 cm.); orange-yellow with pink tints, later creamy white; fragrant

**GROWTH:** 7–10 ft. (2–3 m.) high; bushy

**FEATURES:** Charming climber, almost prickle-free canes; northerly exposures and half shade; winter hardy

**PLANTING:** Pillars, pyramids, arches; shrub climber or ground cover; enchanting as a weeping standard

**INTRODUCED:** Turbat, 1916, France

# SHRUB
# ROSES

With their delicate play of color from pale pink to mother-of-pearl, the flowers of the shrub rose 'Fritz Nobis', which grows to a height of about 7 ft. (2 m.), are an endless source of fascination. 'Fritz Nobis' is also classified as a park rose.

# SHRUB ROSES

### Shrub roses and their characteristics

As their name implies, shrub roses have bushy growth with stiff upright or arching canes, reaching an overall height of 4–10 ft. (1.2–3 m.). Varieties with long, flexible canes are also suitable as climbing roses on obelisks and pillars. An important difference is their flowering rhythm. Most Modern shrub roses flower more frequently than their predecessors, some even continuously. Others flower only once, usually in early summer, and follow this in the fall with another fascinating spectacle, their hips. The blossoms can be in every shape, size, and color known to the species: single, half filled, densely filled, the whole spectrum. Modern ornamental shrub roses, however, tend to follow the trend of the day. Although back in the heyday of the hybrid Teas, shrub roses also had to have their huge, brilliantly colored flowers, nowadays old-fashioned, romantic blossoms are all the rage.

**PAGES 92–3**

When the end of May approaches, owners of 'Pink Nevada' may feel their hearts leap. With its sweet-scented, pink flowers, this inviting park rose, a sport from 'Nevada' (see pp. 100–101), appears particularly romantic in this natural setting, among a host of blue cornflowers.

**WHAT ARE PARK ROSES?**

Sports from wild roses that still have much of the natural charm of their forebears, i.e. need little or no care, are extremely winter hardy, and because of their nicely tailored form and substantial size call out for being planted individually in larger yards or by fences, are commonly known as park roses. Many have single or half-filled flowers and flower only once, but have such a rich array of hips in the fall that it almost comes as a surprise.

Recurrent old-fashioned shrub roses make marvelous backgrounds for beds. Here, the densely filled, fragrant blossoms of the English rose 'Graham Thomas' (p. 113) look down over blue catmint (*Nepeta* × *faassenii*).

## The latest trend: Modern old-fashioned roses

Modern ornamental shrub roses are currently enjoying an enormous comeback, which began with English roses. These varieties, grown by England's David Austin, inspire enthusiasm because they are recurrent bloomers and because the colors, shapes, and fragrance of the flowers have the old-fashioned flair of Old roses. This success has led growers worldwide to create their own varieties, combining a decorative but not too heavy growth, romantic flower shapes, fragrance, and wonderful color play with recurrent blooming, winter hardiness, and robust health. Many of these roses also form part of specially named series created by individual growers, such as 'Romantica roses' (Meilland), 'Fairy Tale roses' (Kordes), 'Nostalgic Flower Dreams' (Tantau), 'Souvenirs of Love', 'Painters' roses' (Delbard), 'Old Master roses' (Rosen-Union), etc.

## Pruning once-flowering shrub roses

Modern once-flowering shrub roses do not need to be pruned. Older plants, however, need to be thinned out once a year to remove dead, sick, or frozen canes.

## Pruning recurrent shrub roses

Modern recurrent shrub roses flower first on the current year's wood and subsequently on the newly developing laterals on the canes on which they have withered. Pruning early in the year is essential to ensure nice, controlled growth and good flowering. To do this, remove one or two aged canes at their base and shorten the others. Strong canes should be cut back by one-third and weak canes by two-thirds. In order to ensure that all the canes get as much light as possible, the silhouette of the rose after being pruned should resemble a layered pyramid.

# 'SCHNEE-WITTCHEN®'

ORNAMENTAL SHRUB ROSE / Synonyms: 'Iceberg', 'Fée des Neiges'

From June, when the graceful flowers of this rose open in clusters from rose-tinted buds, the yard itself glows on gloomy days. 'Schneewittchen®' will then flower conscientiously until first frost, showing that it can tolerate heat. Its rain-resistant blossoms take on a pink shimmer in cooler weather. Because the rose itself is prone to black spot, it needs the best possible planting conditions. It reveals its fairy-tale charm when planted beside violet and pastel-colored companions or in white and yellow combinations, but especially as a standard in the middle of a flowerbed or as 'Climbing Schneewittchen', its climber sport, up a climbing support.
In order to ensure a profuse later flush, it should be deadheaded by removing withered clusters directly above the first fully formed leaf below.

**FLOWERING:** Recurrent; half-filled; large; Ø 3 in. (8 cm.); white; fragrant
**GROWTH:** Broad, upright bush, about 4 ft. (1.2 m.) high
**FEATURES:** World's Favorite Rose 1983; suits half shade; winter hardy
**PLANTING:** For beds, hedges; wonderful as a specimen
**INTRODUCED:** Kordes, 1958, Germany

# 'WINCHESTER CATHEDRAL®'

ORNAMENTAL SHRUB ROSE, ENGLISH ROSE / Synonyms: 'White Mary Rose', 'Winchester'

**FLOWERING:** Recurrent; filled; cupped; large; Ø 4 in. (10 cm.); white; strongly fragrant

**GROWTH:** Broad, compact, upright bush, about 4 ft. (1.2 m.) high

**FEATURES:** Robust, suits half shade; winter hardy

**PLANTING:** For beds, hedges; ideal for small yards

**INTRODUCED:** Austin, 1988, Great Britain

Together with the somewhat lower shrub 'Glamis Castle', 'Winchester Cathedral®' enjoys the reputation of being one of the best of the white English roses. Not only does it bring the old-fashioned flair of Old roses to the yard, but it is also a healthy, recurrent shrub rose. No wonder, therefore, that it is a sport from 'Mary Rose®' (pp. 130–1), the pink rose that is one of the most robust English roses. From pink buds, 'Winchester Cathedral®' produces clusters of large blossoms with vivaciously wavy petals at the tip of nicely branching canes. The soft white of the flowers, often with creamy eyes, fits well into any yard. Companions with violet or pastel-colored flowers heighten its romantic character beautifully.

◀ 'Pearl Drift' also dresses in shimmering white and pink mother-of-pearl. This recurrent shrub rose, which grows to barely 3 ft. (90 cm.) tall, but is much broader, is as successful in beds and borders as it is as ground cover or as a specimen. A climbing sport from it, known as 'Pearl Drift Climbing', is also available.

# 'FLORA ROMANTICA'

Synonym: 'Mon Jardin & Ma Maison' / ORNAMENTAL SHRUB ROSE, ROMANTICA ROSE

The full, creamy-white, rosette-like flowers of 'Flora Romantica', which look like little frilly, flared skirts fading toward their hems, light up this shrub magically from the end of June on. Even though it has both fragrance and beauty, the fascination exerted by this rose is not just a close-up affair, however; also from a distance it has singular effect, because of the way in which its colors seem to flow through the light. 'Flora Romantica' can also be planted toward the back of a yard to create a surprise. If the light and soil there are good, its gleaming foliage, which is also fairly resistant to mildew, will thank you. Perfume seekers and romantics can not only plant this rose near a bench but also train it to grow up an arch like a climber.

▶ Nostalgic dreams of roses are also embodied in 'Martine Guillot', a variety created by Guillot-Massad in 1996. The thick clusters of fragrant, white, globular blossoms on this 4½-ft. (1.3-m.) shrub will work their magic through until fall.

**FLOWERING:** Recurrent; densely filled; Ø 3 in. (8 cm.); yellowish; fragrant

**GROWTH:** Broad, upright bush, about 5 ft. (1.5 m.) high

**FEATURES:** Requires sunny, airy position; rain resistant, winter hardy

**PLANTING:** For beds, as specimens, in groups

**INTRODUCED:** Meilland, 1998, France

# 'NEVADA'
ORNAMENTAL SHRUB ROSE, PARK ROSE

'Nevada' is often touted in rose catalogs as a wonderful park rose. The term 'park rose' is used to describe sports from wild roses that still retain much of the natural charm of their forebears. Like 'Nevada', many of them have single or half-filled flowers and do not need deadheading, pruning, or winter protection. Most of them are large, widely spreading shrubs with dense growth, which work best if planted as specimens. All of this applies to 'Nevada' just as much as to its pink-blossomed sport, 'Marguerite Hilling'. Both roses can also be trained as climbers and should be cut right back to about 4 in. (10 cm.) every six to eight years in order to ensure that they retain their flowering quality.

**FLOWERING:** Somewhat recurrent; single; Ø 5 in. (12 cm.); creamy white
**GROWTH:** Broad, upright, widely spreading bush, about 7 ft. (2 m.) high
**FEATURES:** Suits half shade; very winter hardy
**PLANTING:** For semi-wild yards, hedges, as a specimen; by fences, water, and to edge wooded areas
**INTRODUCED:** Dot, 1927, Spain

▼ Although the flowers of 'Jacqueline du Pré' resemble those of 'Nevada' in shape, color, and size, the resemblance ends there. Created by Harkness in 1989, 'Jacqueline du Pré' blooms more frequently and at barely 4 ft. (1.2 m.) high also suits small yards well. It has been awarded the Royal Horticultural Society Award of Garden Merit.

# 'ROKOKO II®'
ORNAMENTAL SHRUB ROSE

**FLOWERING:** Recurrent; loosely filled; Ø 3 in. (8 cm.); creamy white with pink tints; delicate fragrance

**GROWTH:** Upright, about 5 ft. (1.5 m.) high

**FEATURES:** Tolerates heat and rain; very winter hardy

**PLANTING:** For elegant or romantic yards; for beds and hedges; enchanting as a standard

**INTRODUCED:** Tantau, 1987, Germany

This rose spells versatility! 'Rokoko II®', with its romantic, wavy petals, brings a touch of sweetness and elegant finesse to the fairy-tale flair of days long ago, which enables it to fit in just as well in the yard of a country house as in a relaxed dream hideaway or refined city yard. The only thing that is indispensable in all cases is a perfect planting position, with the proper soil and light. The canes can also be trained over a pyramid or obelisk in a bed. Whether as a ready-formed high point or as a free-growing shrub, 'Rokoko II®' should not be planted beside garish or loud companions. On the other hand, it goes marvelously with violet, aubergine, white, yellow, and salmon-pink perennials, as well as plants with beautiful yellowish and bluey-green leaves and grasses.

# 'FRÜHLINGSDUFT'

Synonym: 'Spring Fragrance' / ORNAMENTAL SHRUB ROSE, PARK ROSE

'Frühlingsduft' is one of the most beautiful of the so-called Spring varieties (*Frühlings-Sorten*), which are Kordes roses bred in the middle of the last century from crosses with pimpernel roses (*Rosa spinosissima* syn. *R. pimpinellifolia*). All their names contain the word 'Spring' or 'May' in reference to the fact that they bloom early. If they are in the yard, their sweet fragrance can be enjoyed as early as late May. The lightly filled blossoms of 'Frühlingsduft', with their old-fashioned color play of fine cream, apricot, and pink, often bring fresh delight in a gentle late-summer rebloom. This healthy shrub can be trained as a climber up pyramids, obelisks, and arches, and can then attain a height of about 10 ft. (3 m.).

▶ 'Maigold' is another one-time bloomer of the Kordes Spring varieties. Its apricot-yellow blossoms appear in May and have a bewitching fragrance. The canes of this nearly 8-ft. (2.5-m.) high shrub can also climb up arches, obelisks, and pillars.

**FLOWERING:** One-time bloomer; loosely filled; Ø 2¾ in. (7 cm.); creamy white with yellow center and pink tints; strong fragrance

**GROWTH:** Arching, broad bush; about 10 ft. (3 m.) high

**FEATURES:** Robust climber, suits half shade and wooded areas; very winter hardy

**PLANTING:** For beds, groups, and as specimens; enchanting in wooded areas; also as a climber

**INTRODUCED:** Kordes, 1949, Germany

# 'ABRAHAM DARBY®'

ORNAMENTAL SHRUB ROSE, ENGLISH ROSE / Synonyms: 'Abraham', 'Country Darby'

**FLOWERING:** Remontant; densely filled; cupped; Ø 4 in. (10 cm.); yellowish apricot with pink tints; strong fragrance

**GROWTH:** 5–6½ ft. (1.5–2 m.) high; strong, upright, nicely branching

**FEATURES:** Robust climber; tolerates heat and rain; winter hardy

**PLANTING:** For beds, in groups and as specimens; also as a climber

**INTRODUCED:** Austin, 1985, Great Britain

In June, the large, cupped blooms of 'Abraham Darby®' emerge from round, apricot-colored buds, filling whole areas of the yard with their endlessly varied play of color and bewitching fragrance. Their color, which seems to fade as it approaches the edge of the petals, and their round, densely filled shape give this rose something of a romantic note and the magical flair of Old roses. 'Abraham Darby®' fits in wonderfully at the back of a border or flowerbed, or adds an ornamental touch when trained up a pyramid or obelisk. With its canes, which can grow up to 10 ft. (3 m.) long when supported on a climbing frame, this rose would do honor to any climber when espaliered or growing over an arch. In small yards it can be enjoyed as an attractive, space-saving standard.

◄ 'Ambridge Rose®' also has fragrant, apricot-colored blooms. At only around 30 in. (75 cm.) tall, this small, bushy, remontant English rose is best suited to small yards, flowerbeds, and borders.

# 'SCHLOSS EUTIN®'
## ORNAMENTAL SHRUB ROSE, FAIRY TALE ROSE

Given the shape and color of its blossoms, 'Schloss Eutin®' fits in with the current trend for old-fashioned roses. It comes as no wonder, then, that the nursery that created it, Kordes, includes it in their group called "Fairy Tale roses." Characteristically, all the roses in this group have wonderfully attractive, full blossoms that are reminiscent of Old roses. They flower more frequently and profusely, and are healthy and easy to care for. With their delicate pastel tones, they can be planted as companions for flowers with stronger, darker tones. The louder and more garish these colors become, however, the smaller the number of plants that should be used. For their companions are there not to compete with the fragrant rose blossoms or overwhelm them, but to accompany and set the scene for them.

▶ 'Colette' also shares the charm of densely filled Old roses. Its separate, golden-brown flowers appear in sumptuous splendor and give off a strong, sweet fragrance. This 6½-ft. (2-m.) tall recurrent shrub is one of Meillands' Modern Romantica roses.

**FLOWERING:** Recurrent; loosely filled; cupped; Ø 3 in. (8 cm.); delicate apricot with darker center; gentle fragrance

**GROWTH:** Broad, upright, 4 ft. (1.2 m.) high

**FEATURES:** Robust, winter hardy

**PLANTING:** For beds and borders, in groups and as specimens

**INTRODUCED:** Kordes, 2005, Germany

# 'WESTERLAND®'

ORNAMENTAL SHRUB ROSE / Synonym:
'Kordes' Rose Westerland'

Because of its color, 'Westerland®' attracts attention early in the year, in budding season. Its delicate leaves are protected from the sun and are given their early dark red color by anthocyanins, the pigments in plant cells. Later, their leaves change color to a glistening dark green. In common with many other roses, its beautifully colored blossoms stand out against the dark foliage, their delicately scalloped petals glowing in a spectrum of powerful shades of gold and orange. After its first flush in June, 'Westerland®' flowers again, but less exuberantly, and then in fall often blossoms once more, in a second rich flush that can last until the snow comes. During this time its canes are long and soft, and can suffer extensive frost damage, but after being cut back in the spring the rose will put out vigorous new canes again.

FLOWERING: Recurrent; loosely filled; Ø 4–5 in. (10–12 cm.); yellowish salmon to rose pink; strong fragrance

GROWTH: Broad, upright, strong; up to 5 ft. (1.5 m.) high

FEATURES: ADR Quality Certificate 1974; easy maintenance climber; tolerates rain and heat; winter hardy

PLANTING: For flowerbeds and borders, in groups and as specimens

INTRODUCED: Kordes, 1969, Germany

# 'RUGELDA®'
ORNAMENTAL SHRUB ROSE

**FLOWERING:** Recurrent; loosely filled; Ø 3½ in. (9 cm.); yellow with red border; fragrant.

**GROWTH:** Strong, upright, bushy; up to 6½ ft. (2 m.) high

**FEATURES:** ADR Quality Certificate 1992; healthy; tolerates half shade; very winter hardy

**PLANTING:** At the back of flowerbeds and borders, in groups and as specimens; ideal for thick hedges

**INTRODUCED:** Kordes, 1989, Germany

The recurrent shrub rose 'Rugelda®' could be described as the embodiment of vitality. In June, its opening blossoms look as if they have been playing too close to the fire, for they have a red border all around their edges. With that, a play of color starts that lasts until fall. Close to red, hybrid Tea-like buds, clusters of large flowers open that vary in tone from orange to gold; with the passing days and weeks, they will fade to lemon yellow, drawing the eye to the orange tassels of their stamens. Because each of these phases in the development of the flowers is worth watching as it occurs, 'Rugelda®' has an effect that is both cheerful and lively. A bushy shrub with thick canes, it is also very prickly and quickly grows to form an impenetrable hedge 6½ ft. (2 m.) high. In the spring its canes should be cut back by one-third.

◀ 'Bonanza' gives a similar impression of being full of joie de vivre. Its loosely filled blossoms recall the jaunty, flounced dresses that ladies used to wear in the saloons of the Old West. This 6½-ft. (2-m.) recurrent shrub rose, which was awarded a quality certificate by the ADR, has bright yellow flowers with red borders.

# 'JOSEPH'S COAT®'
## ORNAMENTAL SHRUB ROSE

When 'Joseph's Coat®' opens in clusters of large flowers in June, it is as if a multicolored display of fireworks has been started. From dark red buds the flowers open, their rose pink emerging from a fiery orange center before gradually fading to orange and even lighter gold, making the rose spectacularly colorful. Because of its prickly canes and thick growth, a line of bushes of this variety can grow into a formidable hedge. Yet 'Joseph's Coat®' can also be very attractive at the back of a mixed border, if planted to create tonal combinations with yellow, orange, and carmine companions. In small, sunny places or yards, the 10 ft. (3 m.) canes of this rose will enable it to climb obelisks, pyramids, arches, or small espaliers.

**FLOWERING:** Recurrent; loosely filled; Ø 4 in. (10 cm.); cherry red, flame orange, and golden yellow; enchanting fragrance

**GROWTH:** Upright, arching, up to 6½ ft. (2 m.) high

**FEATURES:** Suitable as a climber; can also be container grown; needs winter protection

**PLANTING:** At the back of flowerbeds and borders, in groups, as specimens, and for hedges; also as a climber and on banks

**INTRODUCED:** Armstrong & Swim, 1964, USA

# 'LICHTKÖNIGIN LUCIA®'

ORNAMENTAL SHRUB ROSE / Synonyms:
'Lucia', 'Reine Lucia'

'Lichtkönigin Lucia®' is the classical grande
dame of yellow shrub roses. This compact,
bushy plant flowers profusely but is neither
prissy nor sensitive. In June its dull yellow
buds, which resemble those of hybrid Teas,
open into lightly filled, long-lasting blooms
growing on short, strong canes. Gradually
they fade into a pastel lemon yellow, which,
when seen against the dark foliage beneath,
gives the rose a powerful effect at a distance.
'Lichtkönigin Lucia®' provides a luminous
background to flowerbeds and borders
that harmonizes with virtually every color.
When planted together with summer sage
(*Salvia nemorosa*), the combined effect of all
their shades can be seen here; that of their
fragrances and scents must be experienced.

**FLOWERING:** Recurrent; filled; Ø 3½ in. (9 cm.);
strong lemon yellow; light fragrance
**GROWTH:** Bolt upright, bushy; 5 ft. (1.5 m.) high
**FEATURES:** ADR Quality Certificate 1968; easy-
maintenance climber; rain resistant; tolerates heat;
very winter hardy
**PLANTING:** For flowerbeds, borders, hedges; lovely in
groups and as specimens
**INTRODUCED:** Kordes, 1966, Germany

# 'DOUBLE YELLOW'

ORNAMENTAL SHRUB ROSE

**FLOWERING:** One-time; half filled; Ø 2½ in. (6 cm.); light yellow; delicate fragrance

**GROWTH:** Arching, 4 ft. (1.2 m.) high

**FEATURES:** Flowers in May; robust; tolerates half shade; strong runner formation; very winter hardy

**PLANTING:** For semi-wild yards, as specimens, in groups or hedges

**INTRODUCED:** Williams, 1828, Great Britain

Yellow on yellow, this companion planting attracts the rays of the spring sun. From mid-May onward, the half-filled blossoms of this once-flowering Old shrub rose, together with yellow corydalis (*Pseudofumaria lutea*) and Welsh poppy (*Meconopsis cambrica*) at its feet, form a joyous gathering. Close to this natural rose are other, very similar varieties that also flower at the end of May and often produce black hips as well, an unmistakable sign that they all have Pimpernel rose blood in their veins. Such very similar varieties include 'Williams' Double Yellow', which was bred in 1828 by Williams in Great Britain, and *Rosa × harisonii* (synonyms: 'The Yellow Rose of Texas', 'Harison's Yellow', 'Yellow Sweet Brier'), which was discovered in G. H. Harison's yard in New York in 1830.

◀ 'Canary Bird' also has lots of unaffected charm. Its plain sun-yellow blossoms start to open as early as the beginning of May, while in the fall its long, arching canes (this rose can grow to some 6½ ft./2 m.) are laden with black hips.

# 'THE PILGRIM'

Synonym: 'Gartenarchitekt Günther Schulze' / ORNAMENTAL SHRUB ROSE, ENGLISH ROSE

Yellow roses are almost always somewhat more sensitive and demanding than other roses; this makes 'The Pilgrim' the more noteworthy. With its silky blooms, which fade toward the edges into something ethereal, this is without doubt not only one of the most beautiful of all the English roses, but also one of the most reliable, provided that it is given optimal growing conditions in terms of soil and light. Because its canes are very slender and tight, it is advisable to plant two or three of these roses together, if possible. When planted in beds and borders, it fits in nicely, its color harmonizing with just about every other shade, but it should not be among too many loud-colored companions or its effect will be compromised. This delicate beauty has another peculiarity: its blossoms occasionally grow right on its canes.

**FLOWERING:** Recurrent; densely filled; 2½ in. (6 cm.); pale yellow, fading to its edges; fragrant
**GROWTH:** Bolt upright; 3¼ ft. (1 m.) high
**FEATURES:** Flowers profusely; needs winter protection
**PLANTING:** For small yards and town yards; in beds and borders; as specimens or in groups
**INTRODUCED:** Austin, 1991, Great Britain

▶ The pure yellow, rich flush, and luxurious hybrid-Tea fragrance of its cupped blossoms explain why 'Graham Thomas' is the most sought-after English rose. This variety, which grows to about 4 ft. (1.2 m.), can even be trained as a climber.

# 'BUFF BEAUTY'
ORNAMENTAL SHRUB ROSE

The attractive ways in which 'Buff Beauty' allows its long canes to be trained can be seen here, where it adorns the guardrail of a small bridge. The changing apricot tones of its blossoms when set against the yellow of 'Albéric Barbier' (to the left of the bridge) are very effective. When the large clusters of this favorite hybrid Musk open in June, its loose, round blooms glow buff-orange before slowly fading, as if they were trying to tint their lives with yellowish ivory. Because 'Buff Beauty' blooms uninterruptedly until fall, it is a real feast for the eye and is best suited beside beguiling eye-catchers already on show. In cold regions, it needs careful protection in winter.

FLOWERING: Recurrent; densely filled; Ø 3½ in. (9 cm.); apricot to bright yellow; enchanting fragrance
GROWTH: 5 ft. (1.5 m.) high; arching
FEATURES: Tolerates half shade; suitable for cultivation as a climber and in a container; needs winter protection
PLANTING: At the back of beds and borders; as a specimen, in groups or as a hedge; as a climber and on banks
INTRODUCED: Pemberton (or Bentall), 1939 (possibly also in 1919), Great Britain

▼ The large, cupped, fragrant blossoms of 'Charles Austin' (synonym: 'Charming Apricot') are also of a slowly fading, magical apricot-orange; it usually has a second flush as well. As the canes of this English rose grow to some 5 ft. (1.5 m.), it can be trained as a climber. If it is to be kept as a bush, however, it should be cut back by about half early in the year.

# 'BISCHOFSSTADT PADERBORN®'

ORNAMENTAL SHRUB ROSE / Synonyms: 'Kordes' Rose Bischofsstadt Paderborn', 'Fire Pillar'

**FLOWERING:** Recurrent; single to half filled; Ø 3 in. (8 cm.); scarlet; fragrant

**GROWTH:** 6 ft. (1.8 m.) high; upright; bushy, well branched

**FEATURES:** ADR Quality Certificate 1968; robust climber; suits being grown in a container; winter hardy

**PLANTING:** At the back of flowerbeds and borders; as a specimen or in a group; suitable for hedges; can be grown in a container

**INTRODUCED:** Kordes, 1964, Germany

The rich flush of fiery, brick-red blooms produced by this recurrent shrub rose produces a singular effect, not just close by but also at a distance. With its imposing, closed form, 'Bischofsstadt Paderborn®' can be a major decorative element in both medium-sized and large yards, where if planted toward the rear it can be a real eye-catcher, directing the attention to parts of the yard even farther back. In smaller spaces, the choice and positioning of this variety need careful thought beforehand, not just because it demands adequate room, but also because its brilliant scarlet simply makes itself the center of attention and generates a feeling of closeness, so that a small refuge may seem even smaller.

◀ Another attractive rose, 'Scharlachglut' (synonyms: 'Scarlet Fire', 'Scarlet Glow'), has single, scarlet blooms that later fade to carmine. In the fall, as if to console itself for the loss of its single flush, this 8-ft. (2.5-m.) ornamental shrub rose produces lovely hips the size of cherries.

# 'EYEPAINT®'

Synonym: 'Tapis Persan' / ORNAMENTAL SHRUB ROSE

The two-colored blossoms of 'Eyepaint®' gaze cheerfully back at the viewer. This rose has something of an unaffected nature: there is nothing presumptuous about it. In farmhouse yards and sunny front yards, it fits in happily, filling them with a carefree vitality, and adds a colorful accent to country yards. It will flower in large clusters of light blooms, in rich bursts lasting until fall, provided that it is planted in a position where it will receive lots of sunshine but without excessive heat. It also needs the very best soil—loose and loamy with plenty of humus—to help with water retention. If the soil is too dry, 'Eyepaint®' will be prone to attack by black spot.

**FLOWERING:** Recurrent; single; Ø 1½ in. (4 cm.); scarlet with white center and clusters of yellow stamens; delicate fragrance

**GROWTH:** 3–4½ ft. (1–1.3 m.) high; upright; bushy, well branched

**FEATURES:** Suits being grown in a container; winter hardy

**PLANTING:** In beds and borders; as a specimen or in a group; suitable for hedges

**INTRODUCED:** McGredy, 1976, New Zealand

▶ Known by many names, such as 'Stretch Johnson', 'Rock 'n' Roll', and 'Tango', this little rose—it is only 31 in. (80 cm.) high—is another prize-winning McGredy creation. Its blooms range in color from red to orange to yellow, creating an effect of multicolored flame and light.

# 'ROTER KORSAR®'

ORNAMENTAL SHRUB ROSE / Synonyms: 'Red Corsar', 'Korrumalu'

**FLOWERING:** Recurrent; half filled; Ø 3½ in. (9 cm.); dark red; almost scentless

**GROWTH:** 5 ft. (1.5 m.) high; broad, bushy; strong; slightly arching

**FEATURES:** ADR Quality Certificate 2005; easy-maintenance climber; healthy; tolerates heat; rain resistant; winter hardy

**PLANTING:** At the back of beds and borders; by fences; as a specimen or in a group

**INTRODUCED:** Kordes, 2004, Germany

'Roter Korsar®' is a new recurrent shrub rose that stands apart because of the luminous quality of its dark red blooms, making all the others look half hearted. If one intends to plant it by a house, as shown here, one should take care not to place it in front of a south-facing wall, as that would tend to be exposed to extreme heat and dry air, or under the eaves of the house, because there even a variety as robust as this can ail. Anywhere else, it will quickly grow into a yard gem with great clusters of lovely blooms that will not fade even in considerable sunshine. Regular deadheading will spur it to even richer flowering. Its canes can also, if one wishes, be trained up obelisks, pyramids, pillars, or arches.

◀ With its large, velvety, hybrid Tea-like blooms, 'Grandhotel®' is an impressive classic among blood-red shrub roses. This 6-ft. (1.8-m.) high variety, which is also an ADR rose, flowers in bursts until the fall and is very winter hardy.

# 'FONTAINE®'

Synonyms: 'Fountain', 'Red Prince' / ORNAMENTAL SHRUB ROSE

Many people consider that its delicate, hybrid Tea-like buds and blooms make 'Fontaine®' the most elegant of all the blood-red shrub roses. What is more, the spectacle that its flush makes continues throughout the summer because the blooms, most of which come in large clusters, are very long-lived and rain resistant, and flower until first frost. 'Fontaine®' can scorch, however, if planted where the midday sun is at its hottest. When planted as a park rose standard in a large, informal yard, it steps right forward. And if two or three are planted together, its powerful canes will grow together, forming a giant shrub. If, on the other hand, it is to be kept in check in a small yard, it might be placed in the middle of an obelisk and the canes trained loosely around.

▶ Another classic 5-ft. (1.5-m.) shrub rose with velvety blood-red blooms is 'Dirigent®' (synonym: 'The Conductor'). Its blooms, however, are medium-sized and half filled, although they do grow profusely in large umbels until first frost.

**FLOWERING:** Recurrent; loosely filled; Ø 4–5 in. (10–12 cm.); velvety blood red

**GROWTH:** 5 ft. (1.5 m.) high; strong; upright; branching

**FEATURES:** ADR Quality Certificate 1971; robust climber; rain resistant; long canes make it suitable for cut flowers; winter hardy

**PLANTING:** At the back of beds and borders; by fences; as a specimen or in a group

**INTRODUCED:** Tantau, 1970, Germany

# 'F. J. GROOTENDORST'

ORNAMENTAL SHRUB ROSE / Synonym: 'Red Grootendorst'

**FLOWERING:** Recurrent; full; unusually frilly; Ø 1½ in. (4 cm.); carmine; almost scentless

**GROWTH:** 5 ft. (1.5 m.) high; upright; bushy; very prickly

**FEATURES:** Very healthy and robust; tolerates half shade; suitable for container growing; very winter hardy

**PLANTING:** In flowerbeds and borders; for semi-wild yards; as a park rose; ideal for hedges

**INTRODUCED:** de Goey, 1918, Holland

'F. J. Grootendorst' is an unusual member of the rose world with its small, red, frilled blooms like carnations, which appear in giant hanging clusters in June and July and again from August through October. Because of their shape, they were dubbed "carnation roses." Of interest to the gardener is the fact that there is also a pink sport ('Pink Grootendorst') and a white sport ('White Grootendorst') from this rose, the three forming a charmingly colored little group. 'F. J. Grootendorst' is a cabbage rose (*Rosa rugosa*) hybrid and like these is a bushy, prickly shrub best planted as a hedge or to edge wooded areas. Its veined leaves, resistant to disease, change color in the fall to an orangey yellow.

◄ 'Robusta' is a 6-ft. (1.8-m.), upright cabbage-rose hybrid suitable for planting both as a hedge and in a bed. It has single, blood-red blooms that blossom according to the same two-flush rhythm as 'F. J. Grootendorst'. It is both rain resistant and winter hardy.

# 'ASTRID GRÄFIN VON HARDENBERG®'

Synonym: 'Nuit de Chine' / ORNAMENTAL SHRUB ROSE, NOSTALGIA SHRUB ROSE

Its intoxicating fragrance earned 'Astrid Gräfin von Hardenberg®' prizes soon after it was introduced. But its full, round, cupped blooms, with their mysterious red and black petals that seem tinted with violet as they approach the center of the bloom, also tend to make rose-lovers' hearts beat just a little faster. This rose is pure nostalgia, radiating both breeding and nobility, and likes to be treated accordingly, because it is rather delicate. It needs a lot of light without the direct rays of the midday sun, and optimal soil conditions. Ideally, it should be sprayed with a fungicide immediately after the leaves appear. All leaves affected by mildew and black spot should be removed on a regular basis, including those on the ground. To create a compact effect, two or three should be planted together.

**FLOWERING:** Recurrent; densely filled; cupped; Ø 2¾ in. (7 cm.); deep Bordeaux red; strong, seductive fragrance

**GROWTH:** 5 ft. (1.5 m.) high; loose; long, arching canes

**FEATURES:** Tolerates heat; excellent for cut flowers; needs optimum planting position and winter protection

**PLANTING:** In flowerbeds and borders; as a specimen or in groups

**INTRODUCED:** Tantau, 2001, Germany

▶ Another old-fashioned rose, incorrectly described as also having purple tones with pink and white so-called brushstrokes, is the 'Painters' rose' 'Henri Matisse™'. Its breeder, Delbard, describes it as his pride and joy, because it combines beauty, fragrance, and health.

# 'RED EDEN ROSE'

ORNAMENTAL SHRUB ROSE, ROMANTICA ROSE / Synonyms: 'Red Eden™', 'Eric Tabarly®'

**FLOWERING:** Recurrent; very densely filled; Ø 3 in. (8 cm.); dark currant red; intense fragrance

**GROWTH:** 3–5 ft. (1–1.5 m.) high; upright; bushy

**FEATURES:** Easy maintenance; tolerates heat; suits being grown in a container; winter hardy

**PLANTING:** In flowerbeds and borders; as a specimen and in groups; suitable as a climber; breathtaking as a standard

**INTRODUCED:** Meilland, 2003, France

'Red Eden rose' makes romantic dreams of roses come true. With the same, familiar, densely filled, globular blooms as 'Eden Rose '85®' (see p. 128), it has recently become a public favorite. In addition, its gleaming, leathery leaves have good resistance to mildew and black spot. 'Red Eden rose' also thrives when planted in a large container in a sunny location, such as near the front door or on the patio. For very small yards, it is advisable to plant it as a standard, with lavender or honey-sweet lady's mantle (*Alchemilla alpina*) planted at its feet to create an entrancing combination for both eye and nose. This rose can also be trained up an obelisk, pyramid, or pillar to create a high, slender-stemmed point of interest.

# 'FISHERMAN'S FRIEND™'
Synonym: 'Gardener's Friend' / ORNAMENTAL SHRUB ROSE, ENGLISH ROSE

The nostalgic craze for romantic, old-fashioned roses really began with English roses. The aims of their breeders were to combine the shapes and colors of Old roses with the reblooming and robust health of newer varieties. 'Fisherman's Friend™' achieves these goals in a number of respects. First, the variety is reminiscent of the deep, mysterious reds of many Gallica roses. Next, its densely filled blooms, at first puffed up like cups and then later flattening out into old-fashioned rosettes, also have the enchanting fragrance of Old roses. And finally, they bloom with only brief interruptions from June through fall. Unfortunately, the variety is also somewhat prone to black spot and rose rust, at the first appearance of which it needs to be sprayed with a fungicide and the affected leaves removed.

▶ The deep carmine blooms of 'Chianti' give off a heavy fragrance. This once-flowering English rose, which is directly related to the Gallica rose 'Tuscany' (p. 37), is robust and can grow to about 5 ft. (1.5 m.) in height and width.

**FLOWERING:** Recurrent; densely filled; Ø 4 in. (10 cm.); dark pomegranate red with carmine borders; intense fragrance

**GROWTH:** 4 ft. (1.2 m.) high; upright; prickly canes

**FEATURES:** Tolerates half shade and heat; suits being grown in a container; winter hardy

**PLANTING:** In flowerbeds and borders; as a specimen and in groups; suitable for hedges and vases

**INTRODUCED:** Austin, 1987, Great Britain

# 'FRITZ NOBIS'

ORNAMENTAL SHRUB ROSE, PARK ROSE

Rose-lovers with large yards should not overlook 'Fritz Nobis'. With its 6½-ft. (2-m.) high, dense, elegantly arching form, it is the park rose par excellence. Despite its vigorous size, it has a real charm, whether planted as a specimen in a semi-wild or informal garden, by the fence, or as a hedge. Here its salmon-pink blooms and the soft lilac fountains of the butterfly bush (*Buddleia alternifolia*) try to outdo each other in wafting their fragrance toward the edge of the yard. Nor should owners of small yards have to do without this rose, for it can be trained up arches, pergolas, and pillars, and across espaliers, its beauty and fragrance offering the senses a treat that is compounded later when its charming little hips appear at eye and nose level.

**FLOWERING:** One-time bloomer; full; Ø 3 in. (8 cm.); pale to salmon pink; intense fragrance

**GROWTH:** Up to 6½ ft. (2 m.) high and wide; strong; arching; bushy

**FEATURES:** Very long-lasting, rich flush; robust climber; tolerates half shade and heat; rich production of hips; winter hardy

**PLANTING:** As a specimen and in groups; to edge wooded areas; for hedges; suitable as a climber

**INTRODUCED:** Kordes, 1940, Germany

▼ These old-fashioned blooms, with their slightly darker center set amidst mother-of-pearl, belong to 'Bremer Stadtmusikanten®' (synonyms: 'Pearl', 'Elegant Fairy Tale'). This healthy, gold-medal-winning, upright variety grows vigorously to a height of up to 6½ ft. (2 m.).

# 'MOZART'
ORNAMENTAL SHRUB ROSE

**FLOWERING:** Recurrent; single; Ø 1½ in. (4 cm.); pink with white eye; scentless

**GROWTH:** 3–4 ft. (0.8–1.2 m.) high; bushy, arching

**FEATURES:** Healthy; tolerates heat; the blooms have the perfect shape for freezing in ice cubes; winter hardy

**PLANTING:** In flowerbeds and borders; for semi-wild gardens; as a specimen and for pegging down; for hedges and containers

**INTRODUCED:** Lambert, 1937, Germany

The tiny flowers of 'Mozart' never appear singly but always in giant clusters on arching canes from June through October. Small-blossomed and two-colored roses, including those like 'Mozart' with a white eye, are winners in appearance because of the calm generosity of the space they occupy, as can be seen in the yard above. Planted between the uniform green of the hedge and the stone gray of the path, the urn, and the pedestal, the little shrub rose radiates poise and conciseness; likewise the pelargonium in the urn, which is of the same color, is the perfect rounding-out of the picture. This design does not do justice only to the rose, however; the two rose bushes also add a charming touch to the monochrome green and the horizontal bottom of the hedge, loosening and lightening it.

◀ The same color scheme can be seen in the flowers of 'Pink Meidiland®' (synonym: 'Pink Meillandecor'), an ADR-approved rose having the same height. Its blooms brighten from cherry-red edges to pale pink centers, giving this profusely flowering, long-lasting small shrub rose a beguiling charm that is both fresh and lively.

# 'CENTENAIRE DE LOURDES®'

Synonyms: 'Mrs. Jones', 'Delge' / ORNAMENTAL SHRUB ROSE

'Centenaire de Lourdes®' is not just a robust, profusely flowering, luminous rose, but also a brilliant all-rounder when it comes to yard design. As a recurrent bloomer, it can provide a colorful, long-lasting backdrop to beds and borders, or provide a supple, vertical accent growing up pillars and obelisks. As a graceful separating element or hedge, it can divide yards into areas with floral charm. Even in places with impossible soil it can triumph as a shrub or weeping standard growing in a container. 'Centenaire de Lourdes®' has loose clusters of large pink blooms that have a subtle yet busy effect. While their outer petals fade, the inner petals at the center of the blossom curve silkily over the stamens.

**FLOWERING:** Recurrent; half filled; Ø 4 in. (10 cm.); pink; intense fragrance

**GROWTH:** 3–4½ ft. (1–1.4 m.) high; upright, arching

**FEATURES:** Climber; healthy; tolerates heat; rain resistant; suits half shade; needs winter protection in colder regions

**PLANTING:** In flowerbeds and borders; as a specimen and in groups; for containers and hedges; as a pillar rose and weeping standard

**INTRODUCED:** Delbard-Chabert, 1958, France

▶ The large pink blooms of the spreading, 5-ft. (1.5-m.) shrub rose 'Erfurt' continue in full flush until the fall. Because the petals change color on their underside to white or pale yellow, this fragrant rose has a two-color effect.

# 'PIERRE DE RONSARD®'

ORNAMENTAL SHRUB ROSE, ROMANTICA ROSE / Synonyms: 'Eden Rose '85®', 'Eden '88'

**FLOWERING:** Recurrent; very densely filled; globular; Ø 4 in. (10 cm.); pale pink, creamy toward the edge and down into the bloom; light fragrance

**GROWTH:** 3–5 ft. (1–1.5 m.) high; broad and bushy; branching; arching

**FEATURES:** World's Favorite Rose 2006; rain resistant; tolerates heat; needs a sunny position and optimal soil conditions; winter hardy

**PLANTING:** In flowerbeds and borders; by fences; as a specimen and in groups; suitable as a climber and for containers; enchanting as a standard

**INTRODUCED:** Meilland, 1985, France

In 1985, Meilland dedicated this vigorous, recurrent shrub rose to the French Renaissance poet Pierre de Ronsard, who often celebrated roses in his work. First known as 'Eden Rose '85®', this rose, with its full, silky, pink globular blooms that darken toward their center, is the romantic old-fashioned rose incarnate. Because its blooms are so large and heavy that they tend to hang, nodding, on the bush, they can be better enjoyed if the canes are trained over and loosely fixed to pillars, arches, pergolas, obelisks, and pyramids. For all those who think they have no more room in their yards for a shrub rose, 'Pierre de Ronsard®' can also be planted as a standard, ideally in front of the patio, near a seating area, or standing over a flowerbed.

# 'RAUBRITTER'

Synonym: 'Macrantha Raubritto' / ORNAMENTAL SHRUB ROSE

The enchanting little goblet-shaped flowers of 'Raubritter' make one think of tiny Bourbon roses. They first appear late in July, opening singly or in clusters along the previous year's canes; and then they cast their spell, because they are at their peak for a long time, keeping their shape even when their initial bright pink fades into silvery tones. 'Raubritter' is also quite an unusual rose. Its flexible canes tend to droop, so if it is not held firmly in place it will spread out until it is wider than it is tall. If, however, its canes are trained up a climbing support, they can reach a length of about 10 ft. (3 m.), and then its blooms will form garlands. It is also a frost-resistant variety, so it will continue to flower, week after week, taking on the form of a weeping standard and becoming a real gem in the yard.

▶ Its small, loosely filled, puffed-up, pink cupped blooms give 'Angela' something of the flair of a romantic rose. At only around 3 ft. (1 m.) high, this variety flowers continuously until the fall.

**FLOWERING:** Once-flowering; full; globular; Ø 2 in. (5 cm.); pink with silvery tints; light fragrance

**GROWTH:** 6½–10 ft. (2–3 m.) high; loose and spreading; soft canes

**FEATURES:** Not rain resistant; tolerates heat; thrives in half shade; winter hardy

**PLANTING:** In beds and patios, by fences; as a climber on arches and pergolas; as a weeping standard

**INTRODUCED:** Kordes, 1936, Germany

# 'MARY ROSE®'

ORNAMENTAL SHRUB ROSE, ENGLISH ROSE

The lively pink of its flowers gives a hint of the vitality that suffuses 'Mary Rose®'. So even though the clear, modern, bright pink of its large flowers does not quite attain the soft nuances of the Old roses, this English rose compensates through its reliability and robustness, together with a branching, bushy growth that gives it an exceptionally lovely shape. Thus from June through fall, 'Mary Rose®' makes an attractive, almost continuously flowering backdrop or hedge behind lavender borders or flowerbeds, or lightly draped over a fence. Its fresh pink also looks right at home in a farmhouse yard. Grown as a standard or in a container, it always attracts attention, with its showers of blossoms stretching upward and outward like architectonic elements.

**FLOWERING:** Recurrent; densely filled; cupped; Ø 4 in. (10 cm.); pure pink, fading later; light fragrance

**GROWTH:** 3–5 ft. (1–1.5 m.) high; upright; broad and bushy; branching with very prickly canes

**FEATURES:** Easy-maintenance climber; rain and heat resistant; tolerates half shade; winter hardy

**PLANTING:** In flowerbeds and borders; by fences; as a specimen or in groups; for hedges and containers; glorious as a standard

**INTRODUCED:** Austin, 1983, Great Britain

# 'CRESSIDA'
ORNAMENTAL SHRUB ROSE, ENGLISH ROSE

**FLOWERING:** Remontant; densely filled; Ø 5 in. (12 cm.); delicate apricot pink; intense fragrance

**GROWTH:** 6–8 ft. (1.8–2.5 m.) high; strong; upright

**FEATURES:** Needs optimal position or its rebloom will be hesitant; prone to mildew; needs winter protection in colder regions

**PLANTING:** In flowerbeds and borders; by fences; as a specimen or in groups; for hedges; as a climbing rose

**INTRODUCED:** Austin, 1983, Great Britain

'Cressida' is a real storyteller—of rose Fairy Tales of course. In the rose month of June its large, at first almost goblet-shaped blooms open into a rapturous apricot pink that later flatten out into a gently cupped form. At the same time its outer petals fade and reflex irregularly. The delicate frailty of the blooms of this English rose contrasts with its unusually strong growth and long, strong, prickly canes. For this, 'Cressida' has its *Rugosa* ancestor 'Conrad Ferdinand Meyer' to thank, a shrub and park rose that grows over 8 ft. (2.5 m.) high. Small wonder, then, that this daughter can easily reach 6 ft. (1.8 m.). 'Cressida' is at its most beautiful when climbing an arch, pillar, or pyramid, for then its nodding blooms can be appreciated at eye and nose level.

◀ Another picturesque climber, and one of the most highly regarded English roses, is 'Heritage', a remontant with fragrant, mussel-pink blooms. This compact, 4-ft. (1.2-m.) high shrub rose can also be trained up climbing supports.

# 'ROSE DES CISTERCIENS'

ORNAMENTAL SHRUB ROSE, PAINTERS' ROSE

As one of Delbard's 'Painters' roses', 'Rose des Cisterciens' not only shines because it is multicolored, but also surprises because it is the only variety in the group with unusually shaped flowers. Its wide-open, heavily frilled petals enclose a densely filled, goblet-shaped middle that opens only slowly. Inspired by the Impressionists, the 'Painters' roses' are the fruit of much breeding skill and colorful experimentation. In a never-ending play of color, their flowers seem to be made up of short, nervous, artists' brushstrokes. In this way, the blooms of 'Rose des Cisterciens' are all made up of pastel shades of yellow, orange, and pink—and yet no two are alike. Its lovely umbels cast their fragrant spell until fall, even when the rose is planted in a pot.

▶ At just over 3 ft. (1 m.) high, the English rose 'Lilian Austin' puts on another multicolored spectacle, its pink blossoms seeming to glow outward from their golden centers. This healthy, sweet-scented variety flowers until fall.

**FLOWERING:** Recurrent; densely filled; Ø 4½ in. (11 cm.); pastel yellow, orange, and pink; intense fragrance

**GROWTH:** 3–4 ft. (1–1.2 m.) high; arching

**FEATURES:** Tolerates heat; needs optimal planting position, care, and winter protection

**PLANTING:** With companions of different pastel tones; as a specimen or in groups; glorious as a cutting rose

**INTRODUCED:** Delbard, 1998, France

# 'PENELOPE'

ORNAMENTAL SHRUB ROSE

Planted picturesquely between perpetuals and woody plants such as yellow mullein (verbascum hybrid 'Gainsborough') and wormwood (*Artemisia absinthium* 'Lambrook Silver') is the bushy, upright, 5-ft. (1.5-m.) high hybrid musk 'Penelope'. Its large flowers open early in June, their salmon-pink centers gradually fading from the edge inward to creamy white with apricot-pink tints. They have such a sweet scent and blossom until first frost in such rich clusters that Vita Sackville-West once suggested planting a hedge for its fragrance out of 'Penelope' bushes alone. Its luxuriant flush and spontaneous growth give this rose so impressive an appearance that it can stand on its own even when planted among perennials or other roses.

**FLOWERING:** Recurrent; half filled; Ø 4 in. (10 cm.); salmon pink to pale pink, later yellowish, creamy white; lovely fragrance
**GROWTH:** 5 ft. (1.5 m.) high; strong, upright, broad and bushy, branching
**FEATURES:** Romantic climber; suits half shade and container cultivation; somewhat prone to mildew; lovely hips in fall
**PLANTING:** In flowerbeds and borders; by fences; as a specimen or in groups; as a hedge
**INTRODUCED:** Pemberton, 1924, Great Britain

▼ With its breath-light tints of salmon pink, 'Vogelpark Walsrode®' glows creamy white. The red freckles that can be seen are normal rain damage. This 5-ft. (1.5-m.) climber, which has already won its ADR Quality Certificate, has a rich flush in June and July and another in late summer.

# BEDDING AND BORDER ROSES

# BEDDING AND BORDER ROSES

### Hybrid Tea roses—past and present

The year 1867 marks the beginning of what is considered to be the advent of Modern roses. This was the year in which Guillot introduced what was supposedly the first "hybrid Tea"

Beauty and myth surround 'La France'. In the history of the rose, 'La France' is generally held to be the first Modern rose. It has a captivating scent.

(large-flowered rose), 'La France'. So much for the mythology! The reality is that, by 1815, hybrid Teas had already been introduced with 'Brown's Superb Blush'. Hybrid Teas originated by crossing remontant (repeat-blooming) roses with frost-sensitive Tea roses from China. Hybrid Teas are typified by their erect upright growth, which can be more than 39 in. (1 m.) high, each having a tall slender bud at the end of a stem. Large blooms in fine shapes and all colors open out from the bud, which with time became multicolored and more and more dazzling. Many hybrid Teas still produce outstanding scents; others have lost their scent in the breeding process.

The initial boom in these roses came at the beginning of the 20th century, triggering a frenzy of breeding activity. As a result, the roses became more and more temperamental. Around 1945, 'Gloria Dei' was bred (it was originally known as 'Mme A. Meilland' and later, famously, as 'Peace'), which was a robust and healthy hybrid Tea rose; a second bout of intense activity followed during the 1950s and 1960s. Although since then robustness and health have been important aims in breeding, hybrid Teas are still regarded as the most sensitive roses.

Today the preference for romantic, old-fashioned blooms has also had an effect on hybrid Teas; every year new, relatively robust and, in growth, bushier varieties with densely double blooms in soft colors appear.

**PAGES 136–7**

Box hedging brings peace and order to rose beds, and hides bald bases of rose bushes, especially the hybrid Teas. In the foreground, the delicate pink 'Blessings®' (bred by Gregory, Great Britain) exhibits its gossamer-fine attractiveness, while in the border behind, the light red 'Mullard Jubilee' (synonym: 'Electron', bred by McGredy) shows its dazzling color.

### The kaleidoscope of bedding roses

The term "bedding rose" applies to the tireless Floribundas and to the Polyantha roses that bloom right up to frost,

The Polyantha 'Mevrouw Nathalie Nypels' (synonym: Mrs. Nathalie Nypels) is mixed here with perennials as an underplanting. It creates a constant floral border edging the pathway.

both of which have dense clusters of blooms. The older Polyantha hybrids have smaller blooms, no scent, and are generally single or only semi-double. Floribunda roses were bred by crossing the Polyanthas with the larger-bloomed hybrid Teas, which produced larger, often very beautifully shaped semi- or densely double blooms. Today, the differences have become blurred due to breeding—the two classes of roses both come under bedding roses.

The trend for nostalgia is also evident with these roses, evidenced in the bloom shapes from yesteryear, traditional plays of color at the center of the blooms, and extremely delicate nuances in pastel tones—apricot, peach, salmon, and corn tones are currently hugely popular.

Unfortunately, many of the high bedding roses, up to 39 in. (1 m.) high, do not have any scent but, for all that, these plants provide important structure in beds and borders because they lend color and form throughout the summer. Whereas perennials may often leave spaces in beds after flowering, bedding roses provide islands of constancy in inconstant flowering seasons.

## Pruning Floribundas and hybrid Teas
Floribundas and hybrid Teas flower on stems that are newly formed each year. The correct time to cut them back is when forsythia is in bloom. Withered, frozen, and sickly shoots should be cut off completely; all the others should be cut down to three to six buds.

## Above and beyond
For people who cannot find an inch more space in their yard for Floribundas or hybrid Teas, some of the varieties are also available with a slender base grafted onto a standard 36-in. (90-cm.) stem. These can be bought with confidence from a breeder of the variety.

# 'MARGARET MERRIL®'
FLORIBUNDA / Synonym: 'Harkuly'

**FLOWERING:** Repeat bloomer; semi-double; Ø 3 in. (8 cm.); pearl white with delicate pink; wonderful, intense scent
**GROWTH:** Up to 4 ft. (1.2 m.) high; sturdy; upright; bushy
**FEATURES:** Heat tolerant; blooms not always rain resistant; suitable for container planting; occasional black spot; hardy
**PLANTING:** Beds, borders, and low hedges; attractive in standard form
**INTRODUCED:** Harkness, 1977, Great Britain

Anyone who has ever grown 'Margaret Merril®' knows the delightful experience of seeing it in June, when it opens its long, fragile pink buds to reveal silky white blooms, with extremely delicate veins on its loosely ruffled petals, above glossy green foliage. Initially the blooms remain somewhat closed with a hint of pink, which, as it gradually opens, disappears little by little. As with many plants with white blooms, 'Margaret Merril®' is a princess by moonlight. As soon as it is dusk, the blooms not only begin to smell beguiling, but also to glow magically. It is an elegant rose that blooms repeatedly and has won many international awards for its wonderful scent.

◄ 'Isarperle' blooms up to frost in profuse clusters. At 28–32 in. (70–80 cm.) it is not as tall as 'Margaret Merril®', but is just as enchanting, with its extremely delicate pink center, which sometimes reflects warm salmon pink. This scented, very healthy rose received an award by the ADR.

# 'MARIA MATHILDA®'
FLORIBUNDA

The delicate show of the flowers and buds of 'Maria Mathilda®' give great pleasure right from June through frost. As this rose blooms in clusters, which emerge at different periods, the rose color varies from the whitish-pink nuances of the just-opened blooms to the pure white of the fully opened ones. White blooms always have a neutral effect, so this rose may be used in plant combinations in beds or borders to soften up harsh contrasts, especially as the blooms of 'Maria Mathilda®' stand out for their soft white tone rather than a harsh perfect white. They look lovely with lavender (*Lavandula angustifolia*), the peach-leafed bellflower (*Campanula persicifolia*), and also with creamy-yellow *Coreopsis* 'Moonbeam' (*Coreopsis verticillata* 'Moonbeam').

▶ Broad and bushy, 24–32 in. (60–80 cm.) tall, the 'Aspirin® Rose' (synonyms: 'Glacier Magic', 'Special Childes') has been proven to be disease resistant and is suitable for use as ground cover when planted at three to five plants per square yard (per square meter). This rose is a romantic focal point in either half standard or standard form.

**FLOWERING:** Repeat blooming; semi-double; Ø 3 in. (8 cm.); extremely delicate pink; very little fragrance

**GROWTH:** Up to 28 in. (70 cm.); sturdy

**FEATURES:** Suitable for containers; lovely cut rose; occasional black spot; hardy

**PLANTING:** Beds; borders; lovely standard rose

**INTRODUCED:** Lens, 1980, Belgium

# 'LION'S ROSE®'

FLORIBUNDA / Synonyms: 'Champagne Moment', 'Lion's Fairy Tale', 'Korvanaber'

The 'Lion's Rose®' belongs to the group of Fairy Tale roses. This is what Kordes calls the new breeds of easy-to-maintain bedding and shrub roses that combine the wonderful double, old-fashioned bloom shape with robustness and health. 'Lion's Rose®' embodies these breeding aims so outstandingly well that it has already won many awards. Its success is also linked to a social relief project. Proceeds from the sale of this rose will go to support the building of the Peace Village in Oberhausen in northwestern Germany, about 30 miles from the border with Holland. Children from international war zones and crisis areas are transferred there from hospital for further rehabilitation treatment before they return home.

**FLOWERING:** Repeat bloomer; double; Ø 3 in. (8 cm.); creamy white with pink and apricot; delicately scented

**GROWTH:** 24–28 in. (60–70 cm.) high; upright; bushy

**FEATURES:** Rose of the Year 2006; ADR rating 2002; suitable for containers; heat tolerant; hardy

**PLANTING:** For beds and borders; as specimens or in groups; enchanting half standard or standard

**INTRODUCED:** Kordes, 2002, Germany

▼ With its creamy white blooms, which have an extremely delicate, yellowish-pink center, 'Grüss an Aachen' (syn. 'White Willow Glen no. 1'), bred in 1909, is reminiscent of today's "old-fashioned" roses. For enthusiasts of other shades, 'Grüss an Aachen' is available in white or pink.

# 'FRIESIA®'

FLORIBUNDA / Synonyms: 'Fresia', 'Korresia', 'Sunsprite'

**FLOWERING:** Repeat bloomer; semi-double; Ø 2½–3 in. (6–7 cm.); golden yellow; intense, sweet scent
**GROWTH:** 24 in. (60 cm.) high; upright; bushy
**FEATURES:** Withstands rain; heat tolerant; suitable for containers; hardy
**PLANTING:** For beds, borders, and low hedging; attractive in standard form
**INTRODUCED:** Kordes, 1973, Germany

'Friesia®' is a reliable classic among yellow bedding roses that can be recommended to any beginner. This easy-to-maintain rose is wholly uncomplicated and begins to bloom in abundance from early June. Rose beds planted purely with 'Friesia®' have a dreamy fragrance about them, which toward evening will spread to other areas of the yard on the breeze. When mixed with lavender, the colors and scents are interwoven to achieve a nostalgic bouquet. This fairly small rose creates a dazzling yard impression when planted in picturesque borders with torch lilies or red-hot pokers (kniphofia hybrids) in yellow, orange, or red. If planting in rows, plant at intervals of 16 in. (40 cm.); if planting a larger area, use five to six plants per square yard (square meter).

◀ In 1985 the 2-ft. (60-cm.) high bedding rose 'Goldener Sommer '83' (synonym: 'Noaasom') received an ADR rating. It features blooms that are large, loosely double, and a dazzling mimosa-yellow color. When fully open, the petals are reflexed and lighter at the edges.

# 'GOLDSCHATZ II®'

Synonym: 'Castle Howard Tercentenary' / FLORIBUNDA

This yellow bedding rose has a beguiling fragrance, especially when its large, cupped blooms are fully open. Then the outer petals, which are initially an intense, deep yellow color, look almost transparent and make an even more delicate contrast with its dark green, glossy, almost leathery, foliage. The masses of orange-yellow stamens go wonderfully with the almost translucent sunny tone of the blooms. The effect is most powerful when the roses are planted together in large groups; its broad bushy growth habit suits mass plantings. Use about five to seven plants per square yard (square meter). However, 'Goldschatz®' can be a gem worthy of any yard if planted as a specimen in mixed beds.

**FLOWERING:** Repeat bloomer; semi-double; Ø 4–5 in. (10–12 cm.); has an almost transparent effect in the light; sweet smelling

**GROWTH:** 28–36 in. (70–90 cm.) high; upright; broad and bushy

**FEATURES:** Especially lovely in sunlight; heat tolerant; very stable color; hardy

**PLANTING:** For beds, borders, and edging; specimen or in groups

**INTRODUCED:** Tantau, 1996, Germany

**OTHER SYNONYMS:** 'Golden Jet', 'Tresoro d'Oro', 'Tantasch'

# 'AMBER QUEEN®'

FLORIBUNDA / Synonyms: 'Prinz Eugen von Savoyen', 'Harroony'

**FLOWERING:** Repeat bloomer; loosely double; Ø 3 in. (7–8 cm.); golden orange to amber yellow; lightly scented

**GROWTH:** 16–24 in. (40–60 cm.) high; upright; bushy

**FEATURES:** Multi-award winner; lovely foliage; heat tolerant; suitable for containers

**PLANTING:** For beds and borders; singly, in groups, or mass planting; enchanting standard rose

**INTRODUCED:** Harkness, 1984, Great Britain

In 1984, the year 'Amber Queen®' was introduced, and was named Rose of the Year in England. This award was followed by further international recognition; for example, it was named Golden Rose of the Hague in 1991. This variety is fascinating for the delightful shape and color of its gorgeous masses of blooms, which stand out attractively against very decorative, healthy foliage. The budding leaves are initially bronze-green, turning dark green and shiny. The blooms also change color, becoming brighter with time. This rose is a relatively low grower but remains compact and bushy. If growing in a container, place two to three plants together, depending on the size of the tub, and cut the shoots all round it in layers.

# 'APRIKOLA®'

Synonym: 'Apricot Vigorosa' / FLORIBUNDA

'Aprikola®', with its two-tone changing colors, is not just doubly beautiful, but is also doubly good because of its sturdiness and health. For this it has already won numerous awards, including the Golden Rose of the Hague in 2005. In June the plump, orange-yellow buds open out to reveal clusters of initially intense apricot-yellow blooms. As they come into full bloom, the outer petals fold back slightly and take on a delicate pink tone. If there is no space in the yard for extensive rose planting, 'Aprikola®' may be set in a tub as a standard or half-standard rose with white sweet alyssum (*Lobularia maritima*) or blue lobelia (*Lobelia erinus*) planted beneath.

**FLOWERING:** Repeat bloomer; loosely double; Ø 2½ in. (6 cm.); apricot yellow with delicate pink; fruity scent

**GROWTH:** 28–32 in. (70–80 cm.) high; upright; bushy

**FEATURES:** ADR certificate 2001; very healthy; rain resistant; tolerates heat and semi-shade; suitable for containers; hardy

**PLANTING:** For beds, borders, and low hedging; attractive as a standard or half standard

**INTRODUCED:** Kordes, 2000, Germany

▶ 'Apricot Nectar' also has apricot nuances. Its blooms reach anything up to 4 in. (10 cm.) in diameter; they exude a delicate fragrance and bloom profusely in fall. This bushy, up to 32-in. (80-cm.) high rose is also robust and healthy.

# 'MARIE CURIE'

FLORIBUNDA

Synonyms: 'Romantic Dreams', 'Umilo'

'Marie Curie' is a dainty bedding rose, just 16–24 in. (40–60 cm.) high with medium-sized blooms. For all that it has a flamboyant effect, as its flowers are densely clustered, sometimes with five or even seven together, making for an impressive show despite their delicate pastel formality. They are rich in contrasts, standing out not only against their shiny, dark green foliage, which promises a good healthy plant, but also for the carmine-red buds that peep out between the blooms. The blooms are round and very uniform in shape. They open to a relatively flat saucer shape and the wavy edges of the outer petals give the impression of vigorous movement. The center takes on an intensely hot shade, whereas the outer petals are a delicate silky shade of pink.

**FLOWERING:** Repeat bloomer; semi-double; Ø 2–2½ in. (5–6 cm.); copper yellow to golden brown with pink blush; fragrant

**GROWTH:** 16–24 in. (40–60 cm.) high; strong; upright; bushy

**FEATURES:** Rain resistant; heat tolerant; suitable for containers; hardy

**PLANTING:** For beds and borders; specimens, in groups and extensive planting; attractive standard and lovely cut flower for the house

**INTRODUCED:** Meilland, 1997, France

# 'GEBRÜDER GRIMM®'

FLORIBUNDA / Synonyms: 'Joli Tambour', 'Eternal Flame'

**FLOWERING:** Repeat bloomer; fully double; Ø 3 in. (7 cm.); brilliant orange with peachy yellow, later pink; delicate fragrance

**GROWTH:** 28–32 in. (70–80 cm.) high; upright

**FEATURES:** ADR rating 2002; very healthy beginner's rose; moderate rain resistance; heat and partial shade tolerant; hardy

**PLANTING:** For flowerbeds and borders; specimens or in groups; splendid colorful standard

**INTRODUCED:** Kordes, 2002, Germany

**OTHER SYNONYMS:** 'Brothers Grimm Fairy Tale', 'Gremlin', 'Korassenet'

This bedding rose combines all the charm of modern trends for "old-fashioned" flower beauty with exceptionally healthy leaves. The spores of the rose grower's worst nightmare diseases, such as black spot and mildew, have difficulty gaining a foothold on the shiny, dark green leaves, so this variety is amazingly healthy. The bloom exhibits all the distinguishing features of a Floribunda, i.e. color and reflexed yellow reverses of the outer petals, but with its fully double shape and lightly waving petal edges it is reminiscent of an old garden rose. Its fresh, vivid orange shade fades with time to a soft pink. If using 'Gebrüder Grimm®' in a border, plant 16–20 in. (40–50 cm.) apart.

# 'SANGERHÄUSER JUBILÄUMSROSE®'

Synonyms: 'Cervia', 'Floral Fairy Tale' / FLORIBUNDA

This bedding rose has the fashionable soft apricot tones of an "old-fashioned" rose. The blooms unfold to a flat form, almost reminiscent of a species rose. Whereas in the center the petal tones are predominantly yellowish to salmon pink, the color intensity fades at the petal edges and later takes on a delicate pink hue. The 'Sangerhäuser Jubiläumsrose®' is attractive for its delicate nuances but, more than that, for its abundant blooming qualities. Its soft tones harmonize well with other flower colors, such as the blue or violet shades of cranesbill (*Geranium*), the lime-green of lady's mantle (*Alchemilla*) or the pale yellow of Jerusalem sage (*Phlomis russeliana*).

**FLOWERING:** Repeat bloomer; fully double; Ø 3 in. (8 cm.); delicate apricot to delicate pink; scented

**GROWTH:** 28 in. (70 cm.) high; moderately strong; upright; bushy

**FEATURES:** For beginners; heat tolerant; suitable for containers; hardy

**PLANTING:** For flowerbeds and borders; excellent standard or half standard

**INTRODUCED:** Kordes, 2003, Germany

**OTHER SYNONYMS:** 'Kormamtiza', 'The Wren'

▶ 'Badener Gold' (McGredy, 1974) features dazzling golden orange tones with soft reddish nuances and large, lightly fragranced blooms. Unfortunately, its glossy foliage can be susceptible to black spot.

# 'CHORUS®'
FLORIBUNDA

**FLOWERING:** Repeat bloomer; loosely double; Ø 3–4 in. (8–10 cm.); scarlet red; no scent
**GROWTH:** 20–28 in. (50–70 cm.) high; vigorous; upright; bushy
**FEATURES:** Withstands rain; heat tolerant; suitable for containers; hardy
**PLANTING:** For flowerbeds and borders; specimens, in groups or extensive planting
**INTRODUCED:** Meilland, 1975, France

'Chorus®' has long been recognized as a top-quality scarlet bedding rose. However, in 1977 its ADR certificate was withdrawn, as over time it was becoming increasingly susceptible to black spot; however, it showed no signs of mildew. Loss of ability to resist disease is a symptom that is often seen in roses that have been in cultivation over long periods. Nevertheless, for those who still decide on 'Chorus®', find it a sunny, airy location in the yard. Bluish-violet combinations go well with its intense color tones, such as larkspur (*Delphinium*) or sage (*Salvia nemorosa*); also yellow and orange flowers such as sneezeweed (*Helenium*) or daylily (*Hemerocallis*) and gray or silver-leaved plants such as mugwort (*Artemisia*) or lavender cotton (*Santolina chamaecyparissus*).

◀ 'Happy Wanderer II®' is a similarly striking rose. At 16–24 in. (40–60 cm.) high, it is typical of McGredy, who likes to experiment with powerful, dazzling colors. This rose won an ADR rating in 1975 for its robustness.

# 'LA SEVILLANA'
Synonym: 'Sevillana' / FLORIBUNDA

With its dazzling scarlet-red blooms that reliably bring splashes of color to the garden from June through October, 'La Sevillana' has been one of the most proven bedding roses for many years, with its sizzling red tones. Although this intense shade is less sought after currently, it is nevertheless well suited for use in creating areas of hot-toned planting combinations. The advantage of a healthy and vigorous repeat flowering rose such as 'La Sevillana' is also that it will reliably enrich borders with color and structure over a long period. Plant them 14 in. (35 cm.) apart or six to seven per square yard (square meter). Incidentally, the pink-colored mutation 'Pink La Sevillana' has proved to be much less healthy. This rose has been removed from the ADR rose list.

► 'Tornado®' (synonym: 'Kordes' Rose Tornado'), a splendid orange-red bloom, also blooms continuously right up to fall. Its clusters of semi-double, dish-shaped blooms open flat and are very rain resistant.

**FLOWERING:** Repeat bloomer; semi-double; Ø approximately 2½ in. (6–7 cm.); scarlet-red; no scent

**GROWTH:** 24–32 in. (60–80 cm.) high; upright, loose, bushy

**FEATURES:** ADR certificate 1979; robust beginner's rose; rain resistant; heat tolerant; suitable for containers; very hardy

**PLANTING:** For flowerbeds, borders, and low hedges; specimens or in groups

**INTRODUCED:** Meilland, 1978, France

# 'MONTANA I®'

FLORIBUNDA / Synonym: 'Royal Occasion'

**FLOWERING:** Repeat bloomer; semi-double; Ø 3–4 in. (8–10 cm.); blood red; no scent
**GROWTH:** 24–32 in. (60–80 cm.) high; vigorous; upright; bushy
**FEATURES:** Robust beginner's variety; rain resistant; heat tolerant; suitable for containers; very hardy
**PLANTING:** For flowerbeds, borders; specimens, in groups and mass planting; attractive as a standard
**INTRODUCED:** Tantau, 1974, Germany

'Montana I®' is considered to be one of the best-quality red bedding roses worldwide. In June its short, dark red buds open out to reveal red blooms, whose brilliance is emphasized because of its usually large clusters. This rose continues to produce blooms tirelessly right up to fall and is considered very useful for providing long-lasting, powerfully colored structure. Though it blooms abundantly, its growth can be stimulated even more by cutting back particularly long shoots before the flowering period at the end of May. This promotes branching, which in turn makes it bushier; as a consequence, it will bloom even more abundantly. The shoots of withered clusters should be deadheaded just above a five-leaflet set.

# 'RED YESTERDAY®'

Synonyms: 'Majorie Fair', 'Harhero' / SHRUB ROSE, FLORIBUNDA, GROUND COVER

Despite its dark red blooms, 'Red Yesterday®' has a really vibrant effect. That is due to the white eye at the center of the tiny blooms, which flower continuously all summer long. The clusters of this many times award-winning rose are quite round and reminiscent of hydrangeas. This rose is amazingly versatile. As a bedding rose it looks attractive in the center or at the back of beds and borders. As a shrub rose it looks good as cover for the foot of walls and hedges; or, as a specimen plant in combination with others, it is delightful throughout its extensive bloom period. Its spreading, arching growth naturally makes it suited as ground cover. Its splendid blooms look stunning when it is planted on sloping terraces and banks, or in pathway borders, and allowed to spread. Three or four plants per square yard (square meter) are sufficient for this.

**FLOWERING:** Repeat bloomer; single; Ø ¾–1½ in. (2–3 cm.); cherry red with white eye; no scent

**GROWTH:** Up to 4 ft. (1.2 m.) high; very bushy; arching

**FEATURES:** ADR rating 1980; very rain resistant; suitable for containers; suited to partial shade; hardy

**PLANTING:** Flowerbeds, borders, hedges, banks; specimens, in groups, mass planting

**INTRODUCED:** Harkness, 1978, Great Britain

# 'ROUGE MEILOVE'
FLORIBUNDA / Synonyms: 'Ondella', 'Red Meilove'

**FLOWERING:** Repeat bloomer; double; Ø 2–2½ in. (5–6 cm.); dark blood red; delicate scent

**GROWTH:** 16–24 in. (40–60 cm.) high; upright; broad, bushy

**FEATURES:** ADR rating 2004; very healthy rose for beginners; rain resistant; heat tolerant; suitable for containers; hardy

**PLANTING:** For flowerbeds, borders, and small hedges; specimens, in groups, and mass planting

**INTRODUCED:** Meilland, 2004, France

'Rouge Meilove' embodies the successful elements of a new rose that breeders strive for—beauty, abundance of blooms, together with a high degree of resistance to leaf disease. Its tough, glossy foliage gives it great resistance to black spot and mildew. Roses with this characteristic combine well with perennials that produce lots of rapid plant growth. The disadvantage of close planting is that blooms and leaves take longer to dry off from dew and rain, which increases the risk of fungal attack. 'Rouge Meilove' shows its fiery displays throughout the summer in pots as well as in partnership with perennials. Plant four to five per square yard (square meter) if the rose is to be used for mass plantings.

# 'RESONANZ'
## FLORIBUNDA

'Resonanz' dazzles with its brilliant orange-red blooms and the charming form of its flowers that keep their round dish shape and flower in large, loose clusters. The flaming blooms look stunning against its dark green, glossy foliage, which is extraordinarily resistant to disease and very healthy. 'Resonanz' blooms from June through October with just a short pause in August after the first main flowering period. If deadheaded straight after blooming to the first fully formed leaf (summer pruning), this will ensure abundant blooms in the following bloom period. Do not prune in fall, as this rose develops lovely hips.

▶ 'Rotilia' (synonyms: 'Korvillada', 'Ruby Vigorosa', 'Red Finesse') is also very healthy, long-lasting, and an abundant bloomer. This rose is light carmine red; it has been awarded many prizes; for example, ADR rose 2002 and Golden Rose of the Hague 2003.

**FLOWERING:** Repeat bloomer; semi-double; Ø 2½ in. (6 cm.); bright red; light fragrance

**GROWTH:** 24–32 in. (60–80 cm.) high; upright; bushy

**FEATURES:** ADR rating 2004; very healthy; heat tolerant; suitable for containers; hardy

**PLANTING:** For flowerbeds and borders; specimens, in groups, mass planting; enchanting as a standard

**INTRODUCED:** Noack, 2004, Germany

# 'RED LEONARDO DA VINCI'

FLORIBUNDA

Synonyms: 'Hilde Umdasch', 'Meiangele'

With pronounced double-cupped blooms, 'Red Leonardo Da Vinci' is the quintessence of a modern "Old garden rose." It combines a vibrant dark red color with a rosette-like, quartered bloom shape that is typical of Old roses. The blooms emerge in loose clusters of three to five per stem, which emphasizes the flat shape and the bloom color, so that this rose is eye-catching from a distance. Happily it is also proving to be very resistant to mildew and black spot. In view of its compact and rather slender growth form, plant at least two specimens in the center or foreground when using in beds and borders. For mass plantings, six plants per square yard (square meter) is recommended.

**FLOWERING:** Repeat bloomer; fully double; Ø 3 in. (7 cm.); brilliant deep red; scented
**GROWTH:** 16–24 in. (40–60 cm.) high; upright
**FEATURES:** Very robust and abundant bloomer; rain resistant; heat tolerant; suitable for containers
**PLANTING:** Flowerbeds and borders; specimens, in groups and mass planting; lovely standard
**INTRODUCED:** Meilland, 2003, France

# 'QUEEN ELIZABETH'

FLORIBUNDA / Synonyms: 'The Queen Elizabeth Rose', 'Queen of England'

**FLOWERING:** Repeat bloomer; loosely double; Ø 3–4 in. (8–10 cm.); pure pink; little scent

**GROWTH:** 3–6 ft. (1–1.8 m.) high; vigorous; upright

**FEATURES:** World's Favorite Rose 1979; robust rose for beginners; rain resistant; heat tolerant; suitable for partial shade and containers; very hardy

**PLANTING:** For beds, borders, and hedges; specimens or in groups; lovely cut bloom

**INTRODUCED:** Lammerts, 1954, USA

'Queen Elizabeth' is a world-famous old-timer with unusually spindly growth for a bedding rose. It reaches well above 3 ft. (1 m.) on stems that have hardly any prickles and, after hard pruning, very few branched shoots. This makes it predestined for use in hedges or at the back of beds and borders, against walls or fences, where its often-bare lower parts can be disguised by herbaceous perennials or miniature shrub roses. To combat the baldness, try cutting the lower parts in layers in spring. Its resplendent, hybrid Tea-like, cupped, pink blooms flower from June through frost. They gradually fade to a light silvery hue and generally hang in high clusters atop large-leaved, dark green, shiny foliage.

◄ 'Betty Prior' is also a high-growing, long-flowering rose that displays single blooms, reminiscent of a charming wild rose, in large clusters borne on stems of 3–4 ft. (0.8–1.2 m.) long. It is also rain resistant, frost hardy, and tolerates partial shade at the edge of woodland.

# 'PLAY ROSE'

Synonym: 'Deborah' / FLORIBUNDA

For those who would like a continuously blooming rose border at very little cost, 'Play Rose' is well worth growing. This is an undemanding bedding rose that is also good in less favorable locations, displaying pink clusters of blooms that may be up to 4 in. (10 cm.) in diameter. As it is well branched and develops broad bushy growth, it is ideal for repeat blooming hedges and as ground cover. For mass plantings, only three to four per square yard (square meter) are needed. The charm of this easy-to-maintain rose lies, however, in its large blooms, which open vivid crimson brightening up to fresh pink. It looks as pretty as a picture in standard form in the center of a bed or at either side of the path or seating area.

▶ The densely double nostalgic blooms of 'Poesie®' (synonyms: 'Jacient', 'Tournament of Roses', 'Jackson & Perkins Rose Poesie', 'Berkeley') are a delightful soft pink color brightening to the outer petals. This repeat-blooming, bushy rose grows to 24 in. (60 cm.) and is very healthy.

**FLOWERING:** Repeat bloomer; semi-double; Ø 3–3½ in. (8–9 cm.); deep pink; delicate scent

**GROWTH:** 24–32 in. (60–80 cm.) high; strong; upright; bushy, spreading growth

**FEATURES:** ADR rating 1989; rain resistant; heat tolerant; suitable for containers; hardy

**PLANTING:** For flowerbeds, borders, hedges; specimens, in groups, mass plantings; attractive standard

**INTRODUCED:** Meilland, 1989, France

# 'SOMMERWIND®'
FLORIBUNDA / Synonyms: 'Summerwind', 'Surrey', 'Vent d'Été', 'Korlanum'

**FLOWERING:** Repeat bloomer; semi-double; Ø 1½ in. (4 cm.); pink; no scent
**GROWTH:** 24 in. (60 cm.) high; spreading growth
**FEATURES:** ADR rating 1987; rain resistant; heat and partial shade tolerant; suitable for containers; hardy
**PLANTING:** For beds, borders, hedges, and ground cover; enchanting as a quarter standard, half standard, or standard
**INTRODUCED:** Kordes, 1985, Germany

'Sommerwind®' is a versatile, classic bedding rose. Its delightful blooms, around ½ in. (1 cm.) bigger than those of 'The Fairy', make it an improved version of that, and it may likewise be used in a ground-cover setting. Whether used in combinations with herbaceous perennials and summer flowers; as a continuously blooming standard in a bed or tub; as a spreading patch of border edging to landscape a terrace; or to lighten up an area beneath trees, 'Sommerwind®' will always catch the eye with its picturesque blooms. It always looks great from a distance, thanks to the color and fullness of its blooms. This rose, however, displays its real charm when seen close up: the ruffled edges of its outer petals give the pastel-pink blooms a fairy-tale touch of gracefulness.

◄ 'Vinesse', a Noack-bred rose, also has an ethereal beauty, which belies its actual robustness and tolerance of partial shade, heat, and rain. This ADR rose 2000 opens orange, turns to delicate pink, and fades to yellowish orange.

# 'BONICA '82®'

Synonyms: 'Demon', 'Bonica Meidiland' / FLORIBUNDA

'Bonica '82®' has proved to be a real multitasker in the yard and is a charming rose that will bloom throughout the summer. When the rose begins to flower in early June, it unfurls from dark pink buds, the outer petals turning quickly to mother-of-pearl pink in sunny locations. As the buds on this prolifically clustered rose do not open simultaneously, they give an exquisite display of varying pink nuances. The delicate blooms belie the rose's frost hardiness, but with some protection in winter it can flourish in harsh zones. It is capable of growing to 5 ft. (1.5 m.) if planted against a fence, and will bloom abundantly there, cascading over the top.

**FLOWERING:** Repeat bloomer; loosely double; Ø 2½–3 in. (6–8 cm.); deep to light pink; no scent

**GROWTH:** 24–39 in. (60–100 cm.) high; dense; broad bushy

**FEATURES:** World's Favorite Rose 2003; ADR rating 1983; rain resistant; heat and partial shade tolerant; very hardy

**PLANTING:** For beds, borders, hedges, and as ground cover; half standard and standard

**INTRODUCED:** Meilland, 1981, France

▶ Even more delicate but not so continuous, instead blooming in flushes, is the 1988 Harkness-bred bedding rose, 'Many Happy Returns' (synonym: 'Prima'). This variety is 28–36 in. (70–90 cm.) high, very healthy, and has a wonderful scent.

# 'LEONARDO DA VINCI®'

FLORIBUNDA / Synonym: 'Léonard de Vinci'

**FLOWERING:** Repeat bloomer; very double; Ø 2–2½ in. (5–6 cm.); dark, 'old-fashioned' pink; no scent

**GROWTH:** 16–39 in. (40–100 cm.) high; upright; bushy

**FEATURES:** Very abundant bloomer; heat and partial shade tolerant; suitable for containers; very hardy

**PLANTING:** For beds, borders, and hedges; gorgeous standard and half standard

**INTRODUCED:** Meilland, 1983, France

This rose has exerted a special fascination ever since it first appeared in public. First, its strong yet soft pink shade, together with its densely double, rosette-like blooms lend it a special charm; and second, it is very frost hardy, so that it can be grown even in harsher zones. A word of warning, though: it is very susceptible to black spot. However, despite that, its popularity has not diminished, and it makes a lovely half-standard or standard rose in small yards, a great container plant placed either side of the front door, or a very pretty display above strawberry or salad beds. Plant the roses 16 in. (40 cm.) apart in borders, or use six to seven plants per square yard (square meter) when planting in masses.

◄ The carmine-red Kordes rose, 'Neon®' (synonym; 'Sweet Vigorosa'), is very healthy and displays dazzling full blooms. This 24-in. (60-cm.) high ADR rose is robust and has spreading growth, making it suitable for hedging and ground cover.

# 'BOTTICELLI'
FLORIBUNDA

The densely double, uniformly round blooms of 'Botticelli', with its ruffle-edged petals, are reminiscent of gossamer-fine powder puffs. Until they have fully opened to a saucer shape, a dark salmon-pink shade dominates in the still inwardly curved center petals, which seems to fade from the outer petals to the center to a very delicate ivory-pink hue. Fully open blooms reveal masses of stamens and display a hint of light yellow at the base of the petals. 'Botticelli' is a delightful yard gem that flowers abundantly in large, dense clusters. Plant this broad, spreading beauty 16–18 in. (40–45 cm.) apart in borders; for mass plantings use four to five per square yard (square meter).

▶ 'Pomponella®' is charming, with pretty little cherry-red pompom blooms that resemble Old roses. This broad-growing Kordes breed grows to 32 in. (80 cm.) high and has proved to have very healthy foliage.

**FLOWERING:** Repeat bloomer; densely double; Ø 2½–3 in. (6–7 cm.); salmon-pink; scented

**GROWTH:** 24–28 in. (60–70 cm.) high; upright; broad bushy

**FEATURES:** Healthy; heat tolerant; suitable for containers; hardy

**PLANTING:** For flowerbeds, borders, hedges, and ground cover; lovely standard or half standard

**INTRODUCED:** Meilland, 2004, France

# 'PAPAGENA'

FLORIBUNDA / Synonym: 'Oranges 'n' Lemons'

**FLOWERING:** In flushes; double; Ø 3 in. (8 cm.); orange with yellow stripes; delicate fragrance

**GROWTH:** 32–39 in. (80–100 cm.) high; strong; upright; bushy

**FEATURES:** Wonderfully colorful; heat tolerant; not completely rain resistant; suitable for containers; protection in winter

**PLANTING:** For flowerbeds and borders; specimens or in groups

**INTRODUCED:** McGredy, 1992, New Zealand

"Papagena' belongs to the group of "hand-painted roses." This is the name for the multicolored striped or blazed McGredy roses. These roses show an exuberance of powerful, dazzling colors that are distributed so randomly as to give the appearance of their being painted by hand. 'Papagena's' partner is 'Papageno®', which was made commercially available by McGredy in 1989. This bedding rose is not so tall, reaching about 20–28 in. (50–70 cm.) in height, and is blazed dark red/creamy white. To maximize the effect of these strong-colored blooms, plant in combination with restrained, monotone plants that will best be absorbed into the color spectrum, or plant with just one other contrasting color, such as blue, to complement them.

◀ The multicolored nature of rose blooms can also be expressed during the course of their bloom periods, as with 'Samba®'. This 20-in. (50-cm.) high Kordes-bred rose opens golden yellow, and on fading the bloom edges turn to bright red.

# 'RHAPSODY IN BLUE'
## FLORIBUNDA

The desire to breed blue roses has been the quest of every gardener since ancient times. The aim is still alive today, though it has yet to be achieved. Up to now the closest breeders have come is to produce mauve- or lilac-colored roses. 'Rhapsody in Blue', available from Kordes, displays the 'bluest' color so far, and at over 3 ft. (1 m.) high, it looks attractive as a shrub rose set at the rear of flowerbeds. Most of the other so-called blue varieties may be found in the hybrid Tea, Floribunda, or patio rose categories. One exception is 'Veilchenblau' (synonyms: 'Blue Rambler', 'Blue Rosalie', 'Violet Blue'), a large-flowered climber that, as with 'Rhapsody in Blue', fades to gray violet, losing its dramatic effect from a distance.

▶ 'Shocking Blue®' is another exotic 'blue' bloom. This 24-in. (60-cm.) high bedding rose opens out its semi-double, 2½-in. (6-cm.) blooms to reveal an unusual magenta hue. It is an abundant bloomer with an intoxicating fragrance.

**FLOWERING:** In flushes; semi-double; Ø 2–2½ in. (5–6 cm.); mauve with white center; scented

**GROWTH:** Around 4 ft. (1.2 m.) high; very upright

**FEATURES:** The 'bluest' rose to date; rain resistant; heat tolerant; requires protection in winter

**PLANTING:** For flowerbeds and borders; specimens or in groups

**INTRODUCED:** Cowlishaw/Warner, 2002, Great Britain

# 'PASCALI®'

HYBRID TEA / Synonym: 'Blanche Pasca'

**FLOWERING:** Repeat bloomer; double; Ø 3½ in. (8 cm.); pure white; no scent
**GROWTH:** 24–28 in. (60–70 cm.) high; very upright; prolific, strong shoots
**FEATURES:** World's Favorite Rose 1991; rain resistant; heat tolerant; wonderful cut rose
**PLANTING:** For flowerbeds and borders; terrific as a standard
**INTRODUCED:** Lens, 1963, Belgium

This extravagantly blooming rose produces slender, high-centered buds in a greenish-white shade that are borne singly or together with just a few side buds on the stems. In June they open their large double, cream-to-pure-white blooms. Gradually the outer petals reflex, and on withering take on a saucer-shaped, rather flat form. On the whole, the flowers keep very well and rarely suffer in rain. Deadhead as soon as the blooms have withered and new, stronger blooms will form. Plant 'Pascali®' roses 14 in. (35 cm.) apart.

◀ 'Polarstern®' (synonyms: 'Evita', 'Polar Star', 'Stella Polare'), a Tantau variety, delights with elegant white, even bigger blooms. This robust variety, which grows up to around 3 ft. (1 m.) high, blooms long and profusely with equally strongly reflexed petals.

# 'EVENING STAR'

Synonym: 'Jackson & Perkins Rose Evening Star' / HYBRID TEA

'Evening Star', planted in a bed at the front of a terrace, will delight for many days, but on balmy summer evenings at dusk its dazzling white blooms and wonderful fragrance will surely enchant. In June the blooms open in a spiral shape from long, yellowish, pointed buds to reveal gracefully ruffled petals. As several may appear on the stems at the same time, they have the optical appearance, in the mêlée of buds and blooms, of enchanting tiny bouquets, sitting atop the large, dark green, glossy foliage. Although 'Evening Star' blooms abundantly, its beauty is of an ethereal quality as it does not do well in rain. In prolonged wet weather its blooms droop and take on a mummified appearance. After the initial bloom period, especially in late summer, it is often affected by black spot.

▶ Creamy-white 'Karl Heinz Hanisch' (synonyms: 'Jardins de Bagatelle', 'Drotting Silvia', 'Queen Silvia', 'Ibu Tien Suharto', 'Sarah') also needs optimum growing conditions, but then its strong, fruity fragrance comes to the fore.

**FLOWERING:** In flushes; double; Ø 4 in. (10 cm.); creamy to pure white; lovely scent

**GROWTH:** 28–36 in. (70–90 cm.) high; strong; upright; bushy

**FEATURES:** Not good in rain; petals drop off cleanly; heat tolerant; lovely cut rose

**PLANTING:** For flowerbeds and borders; specimens or in groups; in white yards, scented beds, and moonlight yards

**INTRODUCED:** Jackson & Perkins, 1974, USA

# 'PEACE'

HYBRID TEA / Synonyms: 'Gloria Dei', 'Mme A. Meilland', 'Gioia', 'Fredsrosen', 'Béke'

**FLOWERING:** Repeat bloomer; lightly double; Ø 4½ in. (11 cm.); golden to pale yellow with pink edges; delicate fragrance

**GROWTH:** 32–39 in. (80–100 cm.) high; strong; upright; bushy

**FEATURES:** World's Favorite Rose 1976; rain resistant; very hardy; excellent for cutting

**PLANTING:** For flowerbeds and borders; wonderful standard

**INTRODUCED:** Meilland, 1945, France

'Peace' is probably the most famous rose in the world and, with over 100 million sales, is also the most planted yard rose of all time. In the summer of 1939, when it was first introduced on Meilland's rose fields for the first time and named 'Mme A. Meilland', it had already received the highest praise. Although the Second World War began shortly afterward, it was taken to Germany, where it was called 'Gloria Dei', and to Italy, where they named it 'Gioia'. When the war was over it was called 'Peace' in the United States. Worldwide, it cast its spell, with its changing coloration and the peony shape of its blooms. To its breeder it was a successful breakthrough to achieving a healthy hybrid Tea, and that ushered in a renaissance in hybrid Tea breeding.

◄ 'Sutter's Gold', when it is fully open, produces color changes reminiscent of 'Gloria Dei'. However, the reverse of the petals and edges are actually predominantly splashed with an extremely delicate red, whereas the insides are light orange-yellow.

# 'ELINA®'

Synonym: 'Peaudouce' / HYBRID TEA

'Elina' has enormous scented blooms carried mainly singly on long, powerful, straight stems. They open from pointed, yellow buds and last very well. They are a pastel shade of primrose yellow at the center, fading to ivory, when the outer petals may reflex considerably. This gives the bloom, despite its size, a fragrant delicacy and the ability to combine with almost all other bloom colors, even the most individual ones, which is seldom possible with bright yellow blooms. More than that, 'Elina®' is prized for its profuse blooming and its dense, beautiful, disease-resistant foliage. Plant 14–16 in. (35–40 cm.) apart.

**FLOWERING:** Repeat bloomer; double; Ø 5½ in. (14 cm.); primrose yellow fading to ivory; delicate scent

**GROWTH:** 28–36 in. (70–90 cm.) high; strong; upright; bushy

**FEATURES:** World's Favorite Rose 2006; ADR rating 1987; healthy; tolerant of heat and rain; splendid cut rose

**PLANTING:** For flowerbeds and borders; specimens or in groups

**INTRODUCED:** Dickson, 1984, Northern Ireland

▶ 'Sterntaler®' (synonyms: 'Abbeyfield Gold', 'Golden Fairy Tale'), a hybrid Tea with healthy, scented 'old-fashioned' blooms, has also won important awards. It is light yellow toward the edges, which may sometimes be mixed with red, and comes from Kordes.

# 'BANZAI '83'

HYBRID TEA / Synonym: 'Spectra'

**FLOWERING:** Throughout the season; fully double; Ø 3–4 in. (8–10 cm.); golden yellow with orange red; scented

**GROWTH:** 28–36 in. (70–90 cm.) high; vigorous; compact and scaly; upright; bushy

**FEATURES:** Robust and healthy; rain resistant; heat tolerant; lovely cut rose

**PLANTING:** For flowerbeds and borders; specimens or in groups

**INTRODUCED:** Meilland, 1983, France

Flowerbeds set with groups of 'Banzai '83' seem to come alight at sunset with the brilliant tones of this hybrid Tea variety. In June the golden-yellow blooms with randomly orange-red edges open from yellow buds with red streaks. They are almost always carried singly on powerful stems and make a great light contrast with the dark green, glossy foliage. This abundant blooming variety stands up excellently to rain and the foliage also shows good resistance to fungal diseases such as mildew and black spot. To create a sunny, scented bed near seating areas or summer-houses, allow seven roses per square yard (square meter). Otherwise plant them 14 in. (35 cm.) apart.

◄ 'Alexander®' (synonym: 'Harlex') tends to have a somewhat more intense salmon-pink tone. It grows to around 3 ft. (1 m.) high and its scented blooms look great at a distance. The blooms often stand in clusters on their stalks, which makes this variety suggestive of a Floribunda.

# 'JUST JOEY®'
## HYBRID TEA

Hybrid Teas are noted for the wonderful beauty of their blooms; whether it be their size, shape, color, or scent. 'Just Joey®' has combined all these qualities in abundance. No wonder then that after winning numerous international awards, it was elevated to World's Favorite Rose in 1994. The blooms unfold deep apricot-orange with gracefully wavy petals that gradually unveil orange stamens at the center of the bloom. As it opens out fully, the blooms fade from the edge inward to very delicate cream. 'Just Joey®' combines superbly well on repeat blooming in late summer with yarrow (*Achillea filipendulina*), the annual, 'Black-eyed Susan' (*Rudbeckia hirta*), and pearly everlasting (*Anaphalis triplinervis*).

**FLOWERING:** Repeat bloomer; double; Ø 4–5 in. (10–12 cm.); salmon pink with cream and delicate pink edges; heavy scent

**GROWTH:** 24–39 in. (60–100 cm.) high; very upright

**FEATURES:** World's Favorite Rose 1994; suitable for containers; glorious cut rose

**PLANTING:** For flowerbeds and borders; as specimens or in groups

**INTRODUCED:** Cant, 1972, Great Britain

▶ 'Lolita®' (synonyms: 'Kordes' Rose Lolita', 'Korlita') also gives a splendid display of yellowy-orange tones. This 28-in. (70-cm.) high ADR rose unfurls from coppery-colored buds to blooms that are golden yellow with a delicate reddish touch. Its beauty and fragrance will delight the senses.

# 'INSPIRATION'

HYBRID TEA / Synonym: 'Inspiration 2000'

The enormous hybrid Tea blooms of 'Inspiration' give an explosive display of color above large, very healthy, mid-green foliage. They look like brightly colored birds of paradise when they unfold from pink buds to tall pink blooms; these appear to be aglow, becoming increasingly golden at the center. This is a spectacle that will captivate in true hybrid Tea style—whether in the yard or in the vase, where they will last as well. 'Fairest Cape®' (Kordes, 2005), which already has several awards, is very similar in color, size, and shape. Both varieties were bred to be healthy and have classic large-flowered blooms with modern colors to make them esthetically pleasing.

**FLOWERING:** Repeat bloomer; double; Ø 4 in. (10 cm.); outer pink, inner salmon pink with yellow; no scent

**GROWTH:** 28–32 in. (70–80 cm.) high; upright; bushy

**FEATURES:** ADR rating 2005; rain resistant; heat tolerant; lovely rose for cutting; healthy; suitable for containers; hardy

**PLANTING:** For flowerbeds and borders; as specimens or in groups 14 in. (35 cm.) apart; makes a lovely standard

**INTRODUCED:** Noack, 2003, Germany

▼ 'Augusta Luise®' (synonyms: 'Rachel', 'Fox-Trot') has similar coloration and a captivating scent. This Tantau breed has the form of an "old-fashioned rose," with flat, fully double petals.

# 'DUFTWOLKE®'

HYBRID TEA / Synonyms: 'Fragrant Cloud', 'Nuage Parfumé'

**FLOWERING:** Repeat bloomer; double; Ø 4–5 in. (10–12 cm.); coral red; delicious scent

**GROWTH:** 20–28 in. (50–70 cm.) high; upright; bushy

**FEATURES:** World's Favorite Rose 1981; ADR rating 1964; scent and cut flower; very hardy

**PLANTING:** For flowerbeds, scented beds, and borders; as a standard

**INTRODUCED:** Tantau, 1963, Germany

This rose is famous worldwide for its wonderful fragrance. It begins to bloom in early June. The flowers usually come in clusters and open from typically pointed oval buds. The initial orange-red of the blooms gradually turns to a lighter crimson shade on fading. Throughout the bloom period the scent is absolutely captivating. These flowers should be enjoyed close-up—in seating areas, on terraces, as cut flowers, or even in rose punch. Despite its leathery foliage, it can be susceptible to black spot and, if it is not planted cleverly when used in combinations, it may have a rather ungainly effect due to the size of its blooms. 'Duftwolke®' may also suffer in midday heat and prolonged rain.

◀ 'Holsteinperle®' (synonyms: 'Heidi Kabel', 'Testa Rossa') is a real eye-catcher with gorgeous rosette blooms in coral red. It has no scent; however, it does very well in poor weather and keeps well in a vase.

# 'TROPICANA'

Synonyms: 'Super Star®', 'Tanorstar' / HYBRID TEA

When 'Tropicana' was introduced, it caused a sensation with its pure salmon-pink tones, which last right through the bloom period, coupled with the classical beauty of its high bloom form. It is no surprise that it has won the highest accolades worldwide. Another plus point is that it blooms with great abundance and happily produces more blooms after deadheading. It also emits a lovely, fruity fragrance and the blooms stand up well in rain. This rose should be planted in a location that is out of the midday sun, as the blooms may pale if exposed to extreme heat and sun. It is also important to plant it in an airy open spot, not too close to other plants, as it is susceptible to mildew.

▶ 'Caribia®' (synonyms: 'Harry', 'Harry Wheatcroft') is a similarly brightly colored rose; however, it is two-toned—the inside of the petals striped red and yellow, the reverses golden yellow.

**FLOWERING:** Repeat bloomer; double; Ø 3–4 in. (8–10 cm.); salmon pink; powerful scent

**GROWTH:** 24–32 in. (60–80 cm.) high; strong; very upright; bushy

**FEATURES:** Susceptible to mildew; great for cutting; hardy

**PLANTING:** For scented beds and flowerbeds and borders; makes a delightful standard

**INTRODUCED:** Tantau, 1960, Germany

# 'BARONNE EDMOND DE ROTHSCHILD®'
HYBRID TEA / Synonym: 'Grimpant Baronne de Rothschild'

**FLOWERING:** Repeat bloomer; fully double; Ø 5 in. (12 cm.); insides deep pink with silvery reverses; glorious, strong fragrance
**GROWTH:** 32–39 in. (80–100 cm.) high; vigorous; tightly upright
**FEATURES:** ADR rating 1971; lovely scent and cutting quality; good in rain; hardy
**PLANTING:** For flowerbeds, scented beds, and borders
**INTRODUCED:** Meilland, 1968, France

'Baronne Edmond de Rothschild®' is an excellent, sweet-smelling rose full of desirable characteristics. Large, attractive blooms are generally borne singly on powerful stems and keep particularly well when cut for the vase and displays. This rose will happily repeat bloom after pruning. It is easy to maintain and very healthy, its very glossy, tough foliage being astonishingly resistant to fungal diseases. 'Baronne Edmond de Rothschild®' will not disappoint, even in harsher zones, where some hybrid Teas are best avoided. When using in combination with other plants, set 14 in. (35 cm.) apart. If planting an entire perfumed bed of this hybrid Tea, use seven per square yard (square meter).

# 'HIDALGO®'

Synonym: 'Michel Hidalgo' / HYBRID TEA

This dark red hybrid Tea is more often used for bouquets and declarations of love than in the yard. However, for those who enjoy a yard with rich red blooms and sweet fragrances, hybrid Teas are hard to beat. 'Hidalgo®', a classic example, can be combined well with other scented plants to make a lovely fragrant planting on a terrace. Plant 12 in. (30 cm.) apart or, for more extensive planting, use nine plants per square yard (square meter). For those who are not so interested in the dark red classics and lay more store by ease of maintenance and health, look for more recent hybrid Tea varieties that combine these latter characteristics with a lovely scent, such as 'Liebeszauber®' (synonyms: 'Crimson Spire', 'Love's Magic'), bred by Kordes, 1991.

▶ 'Burgund '81®' (synonyms: 'Kordes' Rose Burgund', 'Loving Memory', 'Red Cedar', 'The Macarthur Rose') has delightful velvety red blooms that flower all summer, but it is only lightly scented. This rose looks lovely as a standard in a pot on the patio.

**FLOWERING:** Repeat bloomer; double; Ø 4–5 in. (10–12 cm.); velvety dark red; powerful scent

**GROWTH:** 32–39 in. (80–100 cm.) high; very upright

**FEATURES:** Robust; great scent; lovely cut rose; hardy

**PLANTING:** For flowerbeds, scented beds, and borders

**INTRODUCED:** Meilland, 1979, France

# 'INGRID BERGMANN'
HYBRID TEA

**FLOWERING:** Repeat bloomer; double; Ø 5 in. (12 cm.); velvety deep red; scented
**GROWTH:** 28–39 in. (70–100 cm.) high; vigorous; very upright; bushy
**FEATURES:** World's Favorite Rose 2000; robust, good beginner's rose; lovely rose for cutting; hardy
**PLANTING:** For flowerbeds and borders; as specimens or in groups; delightful standard or half standard
**INTRODUCED:** Poulsen, 1984, Denmark

Although 'Ingrid Bergmann' is not highly scented, it more than makes up for that with robustness, profusion, and growing power—and, of course, its wonderful deep rich crimson color, which becomes even more vibrant in the sunlight. In June the blooms open spirally from elegant, slender buds to gradually reveal fully double, high-centered bloom forms. They look wonderful, standing proudly on powerful stems above a complementary planting of violet-blue nepeta (*Nepeta* × *faassenii*), but also in combination with red-white roses such as 'Papagena®' (p. 166) and the summer-long blooms of white gaura (*Gaura lindheimeri*). They also look sumptuous as a randomly placed accent specimens (especially as a standard) in a mixed pink and white planting. Plant 14 in. (35 cm.) apart.

# 'GRANDE AMORE'

Synonyms: 'Walter Sisulu' / HYBRID TEA

Bright carmine red is much easier to use in picturesque color combinations than scarlet red, which is overpowering when mixed with orange or sunny-yellow tones in the front of beds; it gives the impression that the plants are too closely packed together. Such intense, hot-toned beds and borders look great in large yards, but can make smaller yards look even smaller and overcrowded. This is not a problem as far as 'Grande Amore' is concerned. From June onward, when the blooms unfurl from tall, pointed buds to a splendid shallow cupped shape, which then turns to flat rosettes, these roses crown any bed or border with their romantic glory. They look wonderful partnered with blue, violet, pink, or white plants, and will go well with yellow or apricot tones, if they are in light pastel shades.

▶ 'Le Rouge et le Noir', bred by Delbard, has already won many awards for its rose and vanilla perfume. Whether as a 32-in. (80-cm.) high hybrid Tea or as a standard rose, it will bring any yard alight with its velvety dark red blooms.

**FLOWERING:** Repeat bloomer; double; Ø 3–4 in. (8–10 cm.); bright crimson; lightly scented

**GROWTH:** 24–32 in. (60–80 cm.) high; upright; broad and bushy

**FEATURES:** ADR rating 2005; healthy beginner's rose; heat tolerant; good for cutting; hardy

**PLANTING:** For flowerbeds and borders, as specimens or in groups

**INTRODUCED:** Kordes, 2004, Germany

# 'EROTIKA®'

HYBRID TEA / Synonyms: 'Erotica', 'Eroica'

**FLOWERING:** Repeat bloomer; double; Ø 3–4½ in. (8–11 cm.); velvety, dark red; wonderful scent

**GROWTH:** 32–39 in. (80–100 cm.) high; strong; very upright

**FEATURES:** ADR rating 1969; rain resistant; heat tolerant; great scent and wonderful cut rose; hardy

**PLANTING:** Scented beds, flowerbeds, and borders; enchanting standard

**INTRODUCED:** Tantau, 1969, Germany

This well-known, tried-and-tested rose is a classic among hybrid Teas. In June the slender, tall buds, which are usually borne singly on a long powerful stem, open out spirally to reveal large scented blooms. Its dark, velvety, deep red outer petals fold back slightly to reveal a perfectly formed bloom, which is outstanding for its color consistency and resistance to rain. The large-leaved, dark green, dense foliage also proves that it is healthy when planted in the right place. Its mysterious, velvety soft, dark red blooms are just perfect for bouquets, arrangements, and other displays. If the blooms have not been sprayed, they may be used for recipes such as rose sugar, rose gelée, rose punch, salad with rose petals, rose tarts, and so on.

# 'MILDRED SCHEEL®'

Synonym: 'Deep Secret' / HYBRID TEA

'Mildred Scheel®' is an extravagant variety for anyone who wishes for something special, or a "crowning glory" for their scented rose bed. In June the fully double, deep crimson blooms unfold from large, almost black buds. As the blooms slowly open, the outer petals gradually turn from their edges inward to an even darker red, and they have an exquisite scent. So long as prolonged rain does not hinder the blooming, or the midday sun does not scorch the petals, the blooms will flower for an unusually long time. They are perfect for decorations and using in recipes. Mixing with lighter reds or tall purple verbena (*Verbena bonariensis*) helps to emphasize the bloom tones even more.

▶ 'Traviata' (synonym: 'Xavière') is a real stroke of luck for enthusiasts of Bordeaux-red roses. This modern Romantica rose from Meilland combines good health, rain resistance, and frost hardiness, with romantic double blooms, albeit without scent.

**FLOWERING:** Repeat bloomer; fully double; Ø 3–4 in. (8–10 cm.); deep dark red; heady scent

**GROWTH:** 32–39 in. (80–100 cm.) high; vigorous; upright; broad and bushy; branched

**FEATURES:** ADR rating 1978; perfect scented bloom and cut rose

**PLANTING:** For scented rose beds, flowerbeds, and borders; enchanting standard rose

**INTRODUCED:** Tantau, 1976, Germany

# 'PAROLE®'

HYBRID TEA / Synonyms: 'Buxom Beauty', 'XXL'

**FLOWERING:** Repeat bloomer; double; Ø 5½ in. (14 cm.); deep pink with touch of mauve; heady scent

**GROWTH:** 28–36 in. (70–90 cm.) high; strong; upright

**FEATURES:** Award-winning scent; vigorous; healthy; lovely cut rose; hardy

**PLANTING:** For perfumed flowerbeds and borders; as specimens or in groups; lovely standard rose

**INTRODUCED:** Kordes, 2001, Germany

The main aim of hybrid Tea breeding has always been to create something out of the ordinary, whether in color, shape, or scent. To the present fashion for salmon and apricot shades in hybrid Teas has been added a new "old-fashioned" color novelty—mixing color combinations of dark and deep pink with a touch of mauve, and putting them together with 'old-fashioned' bloom forms. 'Parole®' takes up this theme with its enormous, high-formed blooms and intoxicating scent. The display of color is delightful. The newly opened petals are warm deep pink, which brightens gradually to cool mauve pink from the edges. This rose not only impresses with its brilliance and fragrance, but it is also extraordinarily disease resistant.

◀ 'Mainauduft' (synonyms: 'Lolita Lempicka', 'First Blush', 'Peter Mayle') is a similar color and scent marvel. It is a vigorous Romantica rose by Meilland that combines a raspberry-pink color with a raspberry scent.

# 'BIG PURPLE'

Synonyms: 'Nuit d'Orient', 'Stephens' Big Purple' / HYBRID TEA

'Big Purple' is a real eye-catcher in the yard, with large, rosette-like blooms and an unusual color. The deep crimson-purple hue becomes even more powerful on fading. It also stands up well in rain and sun. To enjoy the beauty of the blooms close up, remove single blooms and place in a bowl or in a glass table lantern filled with water to float. In this way the rose will be seen in its splendid entirety. For those who enjoy drying blooms for decorations and potpourri, lay them as flat as possible, with the open flower topmost in an airtight jar in silica gel for ten days. This is the best way to preserve the bloom color.

**FLOWERING:** Repeat bloomer; fully double; Ø 4 in. (10 cm.); deep mauve; strong scent

**GROWTH:** 32–39 in. (80–100 cm.) high; vigorous; upright

**FEATURES:** Rain resistant; heat tolerant; great scented and cut rose; protection required in winter

**PLANTING:** For perfumed flowerbeds and borders; as specimens, or in groups

**INTRODUCED:** Stephens, 1986, New Zealand

# 'ELIZA®'

HYBRID TEA / Synonym: 'Koraburg'

**FLOWERING:** Repeat bloomer; double; Ø 3½ in. (9 cm.); silvery pink; lightly scented

**GROWTH:** 28–36 in. (70–90 cm.) high; upright; very bushy

**FEATURES:** ADR award 2005; robust beginner's rose; very disease resistant; rain resistant; heat tolerant; very hardy

**PLANTING:** For flowerbeds and borders; as specimens or in groups

**INTRODUCED:** Kordes, 2004, Germany

'Eliza®' is very reminiscent of that star among roses, 'The Queen Elizabeth Rose®': large blooms that frequently emerge in clusters, noble, silvery-pink coloration, abundant blooming right up to frost, hardiness that makes the rose suitable for harsh zones and high altitudes, and the resistance of dark green, slightly glossy leaves to mildew and especially black spot. As 'Eliza®' branches well and has a bushy growth habit, it can be placed in pathway borders, with a planting of long-lasting flowers such as lavender (*Lavandula angustifolia*) in front. Alternatively, plant as a small flowering hedge to separate planting areas. Place it in the center of flowerbeds or borders to conceal its base by planting low-growing herbaceous perennials in front.

◄ The salmon-pink hues of 'Aachener Dom®' (synonyms: 'Panthère Rose', 'Pink Panther') lighten to silvery pink; however, the petal edges of this vigorous and rain-resistant hybrid Tea always retain their deep pink color.

# 'MEILLAND'S ROSE ELBFLORENZ'

Synonyms: 'Line Renaud®', 'Meiclusif' / HYBRID TEA

This brand-new romantic hybrid Tea is captivating for its robust, reliable blooming and large, vibrant, fuchsia-pink, "old-fashioned" blooms that are often borne in small clusters. When these blooms are fully open they are somewhat reminiscent of peonies, with petals arranged very close together and, like many of them, they become lighter at the edges. Lovers of perfumed displays will appreciate 'Elbflorenz', not just for its vibrant fuchsia tones, but also for its outstanding fragrance. This strongly citrus-scented hybrid Tea, placed in a pot on the patio or in a scented flowerbed, can be mixed with other scented plants to bring a new bouquet to any perfumed flowerbed. Use six to seven plants per square yard (square meter) if mass planting this wonderfully fragrant rose.

**FLOWERING:** Repeat bloomer; fully double; Ø 3–4 in. (8–10 cm.); fuchsia red; exquisite scent

**GROWTH:** 24–32 in. (60–80 cm.) high; vigorous; very upright

**FEATURES:** Robust; healthy; resistant to rain; heat tolerant; cut rose; hardy

**PLANTING:** For scented beds, flowerbeds, and borders; as specimens or in groups

**INTRODUCED:** Meilland, 2006, France

▶ 'Duftrausch®' (synonyms: 'Old Fragrance', 'Senteur Royale') also has strongly scented blooms of a mauve-pink hue. It can grow up to 32 in. (80 cm.) and has a very bushy growth habit. It stands up very well to heat but requires protection in winter.

# 'LA NINA'
HYBRID TEA

'La Nina' exudes all the charm of an "old-fashioned" rose when cupped blooms open spirally from light pink buds in June. In the middle of the bloom period, the delicate pink center becomes deeper as the outer petals reflex lightly and turn to creamy porcelain-pink. Nevertheless, the bloom retains its round, closed form and, as a result, has a beautifully perfumed, romantic appearance. They usually come in clusters of three to five on a strong, straight stem, which gives the blooms a very abundant effect. The glossy foliage rarely suffers from mildew and black spot; however, care should be taken not to place them too close to other plants, so that rain and dew can dry off quickly.

**FLOWERING:** Repeat bloomer; fully double; Ø 3–4 in. (8–9 cm.); delicate pink; lightly scented
**GROWTH:** 24–32 in. (60–80 cm.) high; upright; bushy
**FEATURES:** Vigorous; heat tolerant; disease resistant; attractive cut rose
**PLANTING:** For flowerbeds and borders; as specimens or in groups
**INTRODUCED:** Meilland, 2004, France

▼ 'Sebastian Kneipp' (synonyms: 'Amoretto', 'Fragrant Memories') displays all the flair of an old garden rose with large, fully double, nostalgically quartered, cupped blooms in extremely delicate rose pink and ivory. It is healthy and has a sweet fragrance.

# 'DOUBLE DELIGHT'

HYBRID TEA / Synonym: 'Andeli'

**FLOWERING:** Good repeater; double; Ø 5 in. (13 cm.); creamy white with red; lovely scent
**GROWTH:** 20–28 in. (50–70 cm.) high; upright; bushy
**FEATURES:** World's Favorite Rose 1985; susceptible to mildew; attractive cut rose; suitable for containers; protect in winter
**PLANTING:** For perfumed beds, flowerbeds, and borders; as specimens or in groups
**INTRODUCED:** Swim & Ellis, 1977, USA

'Double Delight' is a striking, exuberantly scented rose. The elegant blooms are creamy white on opening with randomly mixed ruby-red petal edges. As it unfolds further, the redness increases, and contrasts beautifully with the lighter center. The origin of the name of this lovers' rose is clear — it delights both eye and nose, but seldom the rose gardener. This bushy hybrid Tea is as demanding as it is beautiful. If it is not given the correct location, maintenance, or favorable weather, it will inevitably suffer from mildew. The blooms may also suffer in rain and stick together on opening. That said, 'Double Delight' was named World's Favorite Rose in 1985 for the beauty of its scent.

◄ Two-toned coloration is a popular 'theme' with hybrid Teas. The ADR rose 'Rebecca®' (synonym: 'Renica') has petals with yellow reverses and light, warm, red on the inside of the petals, emphasizing the classic large-flowered bloom form.

# 'LOVE & PEACE'
Synonym: 'Pullman Orient Express®' / HYBRID TEA

'Love & Peace' is rich in color and has a dramatic effect from afar. The reason for this is its classically shaped yellow blooms with irregular deep pink edges, which stand out in stark contrast to the dark green, glossy foliage. The blooms are borne singly, in classic hybrid Tea tradition, on powerful stems, and it never tires of blooming. Added to that, the fragrance is intense, and it stands up really well to rain and heat. This rose can be used as a standard in either a bed or a pot and is ideal partnered with green plants. It will send out flashes of color like an exotic bird of paradise if it is dotted among the greenery. Although it has shiny foliage, should it suffer from any fungal disease, it should be sprayed immediately with fungicide.

▶ 'Jubilé du Prince de Monaco' (synonym: 'Cherry Parfait') has similar-shaped blooms and color markings. However, the colors are creamy white with red edges and the blooms hang in small clusters above the foliage like a Floribunda.

**FLOWERING:** Repeat bloomer; double; Ø 3 in. (8 cm.); yellow with deep pink; scented
**GROWTH:** 24–32 in. (60–80 cm.) high; vigorous; upright
**FEATURES:** Rain resistant; heat tolerant; attractive cut rose; protect in winter
**PLANTING:** For flowerbeds and borders; enchanting standard
**INTRODUCED:** Bailey Nurseries/ Meilland, 2002, USA

# 'BLUE RIVER®'
HYBRID TEA

**FLOWERING:** Repeat bloomer; fully double; Ø 3–4 in. (8–10 cm.); magenta mauve with a darker edge; strong, delicious scent
**GROWTH:** 28–32 in. (70–80 cm.) high; upright; bushy
**FEATURES:** Award-winning scent; temperamental; lovely cut rose; requires protection in winter
**PLANTING:** For perfumed beds and flowerbeds and borders; as specimens or in groups
**INTRODUCED:** Kordes, 1984, Germany

The title of this rose is somewhat optimistic: as yet truly "blue" or "black" roses are not available, and still belong to the realms of fantasy. The efforts to breed these colors have, however, produced, especially in hybrid Teas, some delightful varieties in mauve, lilac, and blackish red. 'Blue River®' is just such an example, with large, beautiful, crimson-mauve blooms, which become lighter at the heart as if powdered, while the petal edges become darker. The blooms are usually borne in clusters and smell exquisite. Whether the rose is planted in a perfumed or perennial bed, its partners should not be planted too close, a minimum distance of 14 in. (35 cm.) apart, as unfortunately, as with all varieties of this color grouping, it is susceptible to black spot.

◄ The ADR rose, 'Mainzer Fastnacht' (synonyms: 'Blue Moon', 'Blue Monday', 'Blue Girl', 'Sissi') has striking lilac-mauve tones and a wonderful scent. This popular variety blooms in great profusion and is hardy.

# 'BARKAROLE®'

Synonyms: 'Grand Château', 'Taboo®' / HYBRID TEA

'Barkarole®' will be assured a place as one of the noblest hybrid Teas with its characteristic slender, tall buds that open spirally to reveal dark velvety red petals that are lightly reflexed and borne singly on long stems. This tall, bushy variety will bloom to late fall without suffering in the rain. In southern locations it may suffer some heat damage in full midday sun. 'Barkarole®' is unusual for its vigorous, bushy growth habit, as most "black" roses do not grow well and are susceptible to disease. 'Barkarole®' is different from the norm in that respect, too, as it has proved itself very resistant to black spot. However, mildew may be a problem, and this should immediately be treated with fungicide.

**FLOWERING:** Repeat bloomer; fully double; Ø 3–4½ in. (8–11 cm.); dark red; delicious scent
**GROWTH:** 32–51 in. (80–130 cm.) high; upright; bushy
**FEATURES:** Top quality variety, popular worldwide; rain resistant; good cut rose
**PLANTING:** For perfumed beds, flowerbeds, and borders; as specimens or in groups; lovely standard
**INTRODUCED:** Tantau, 1987, Germany

▶ 'Black Baccara' (Meilland, 2002), with its deep, dark red, velvety blooms, is even darker than 'Barkarole®'. The darkest of the "black" roses does, however, have no scent and is very susceptible to fungal diseases.

# SMALL SHRUB ROSES

# SMALL SHRUB ROSES

**Three types of growth—one function**
The name used until recently for this group of modern yard roses was "ground cover," due to the special property of covering the ground so densely that the weeds underneath

'The Fairy' with its abundant, graceful blooms is just as delightful as a 24-in. (60-cm.) high ground-cover rose as it is as a romantic standard rose.

could not penetrate. The most important characteristics of these roses are: extremely good health, dense foliage, bushy growth, and constant abundance of blooms sitting uniformly atop the foliage. Added to these characteristics are ability to withstand rain and ease of maintenance. These roses are in actual fact very healthy and frost hardy. This group includes varieties that have very different growth patterns, a fact which tends to irritate some gardening enthusiasts, so much so that they still steer clear of these very versatile roses.

Flat, low-lying varieties form shoots that lie flat on the ground without immediately succumbing to disease. They are normally planted 16 in. (40 cm.) apart or, for ground-cover plantings, four to five roses per square yard (square meter). Varieties that have a bushy growth habit form denser, taller carpets of roses in mass plantings. For these also reckon on planting a distance of 16 in. (40 cm.) apart and four to five plants per square yard (square meter). If the bedding surface area is to be more loosely structured, three roses per square yard (square meter) will suffice. Arching, overhanging varieties have a bushy growth habit and reach between 39 and 78 in. (1 and 2 m.) in height. They form a dense, bushy cover of roses. Planting distances are 20–24 in. (50–60 cm.) apart, and for mass plantings allow about three roses per square yard (square meter).

**PAGES 194–5**
Small shrub roses tolerate partial shade and are ideal for planting beneath or in front of trees and hedges. The shrub rose 'Ballerina' grows up to 32 in. (80 cm.) high and is shown here in combination with lavender at the foot of a small tree.

**INVITATION TO CLIMB**
Small shrub roses with long, supple shoots may also be planted in planting boxes or troughs against a trellis to create a lofty privacy screen.

The bushy ground-cover roses, Lens rose 'Pink Spray' and Lens rose 'White Spray', used here as a luxuriant foreground planting, hide the bare base of the impressive shrub rose 'Rosarium Uetersen®' in the background.

## Talented all-rounders of garden design

Small shrub roses are ideal for banks and slopes, near steps, against wall coping, on terrace slopes, and in the foreground of bedding. They are highly prized in quarter-standard, half-standard, and standard rose form, according to growth habit, and would then require very little space in a bed or in a container.

Most of the more recent varieties bloom tirelessly till fall in white, pink, red, or purple, and they look wonderful in partnership with perennials. Until recently there was a lack of perfumed varieties and yellow- and orange-colored blooms. This was because both the ability to smell and the color yellow are genetically linked with less disease-resistant foliage. However, as the leaves of this type of rose are often on the soil or grow together, the foliage must be particularly robust. Nowadays breeders of small shrub roses have successfully managed to combine both health and scented roses in these colors.

## Pruning small shrub roses

As the primary function of these roses is to spread quickly and cover the ground in order to keep weeds under control, they should not be pruned annually, especially as their abundant blooming remains uninterrupted without pruning. Every four or five years they should, however, be freshened up by pruning them to 12 in. (30 cm.). What is more, not every shoot needs to be cut off. Larger "landscape" beds may be more easily pruned with hedge trimmers or a finger-bar mower.

# 'WHITE MEIDILAND'

SMALL SHRUB ROSE / Synonym: 'Blanc Meillandecor'

**FLOWERING:** Continuous bloomer; fully double; Ø 2½–3 in. (6–8 cm.); pure white; no scent
**GROWTH:** 16–20 in. (40–50 cm.) high; flat to arching habit
**FEATURES:** Mildew resistant; heat tolerant; suited to container growing
**PLANTING:** Mixed beds, borders, and hedges; as specimens, in groups, and massed planting; lovely standard
**INTRODUCED:** Meilland, 1986, France

The full white blooms of 'White Meidiland' look like round scented pompoms. In June they open in clusters of three to five on flat, arching stems. This rose is a sun-worshiper and, although it will tolerate partial shade, its blooms only reveal their true glory in full sun. Then it will flower in great profusion till late fall. It is suitable for combining with perennials at the edge of beds or borders, as a continuous blooming yard planting or as low hedging; it may also be planted in a pot on a column or pedestal where it will trail elegantly over the container. It makes a lovely weeping standard, too, showing the fullness of its blooms to great effect. Four to five roses per square yard (square meter) is required for planting en masse.

◀ 'Pearl Meidiland' (synonym: 'Perle Meillandecor') has very delicate mother-of-pearl to white, semi-double, 1½-in. (4-cm.) blooms that festoon this bush, 20-in. (50-cm.) high, spreading shrub right up to frost if planted in a sunny location.

# 'SCHNEEFLOCKE®'

Synonyms: 'Emera Blanc', 'White Flower Carpet', 'Opalia' / SMALL SHRUB ROSE

'Schneeflocke®' is a top-quality variety of the "Flower Carpet" series bred by the house of Noack. These varieties combine excellent health and abundant blooming with versatility. It is a broad, bushy plant that can be used as a long-lasting bedding rose, as extensive ground cover, or as a cascading, eye-catching standard in the yard. When the rose is fully open it shows lightly ruffled, white petals that have a delicate charm, especially when the light plays upon them. The open blooms reveal masses of yellow stamens and after fading the bloom falls off cleanly. New blooms form amazingly quickly and in addition this rose is very healthy.

**FLOWERING:** Continuously; semi-double; Ø 2½ in. (6 cm.); pure white; lightly scented

**GROWTH:** 16–20 in. (40–50 cm.) high; upright; broad and bushy

**FEATURES:** ADR rating 1991; robust rose for the beginner; mildew resistant; heat, rain, and partial shade tolerant; suitable for container growing

**PLANTING:** For flowerbeds, borders, and hedging; specimens, in groups or mass plantings; attractive in quarter-standard, half-standard, and standard form

**INTRODUCED:** Noack, 1991, Germany

# 'HEIDESOMMER®'

SMALL SHRUB ROSE / Synonyms: 'Kordes' Rose Heidesommer', 'Cerennes'

As soon as its blooms open in June, 'Heidesommer®' becomes a bundle of profuse and fragrant energy that attracts bees in huge numbers. In spite of its unostentatious color, this rose has a vibrant effect, as its small blooms, borne in dense clusters, give an eye-catching display of white and yellow. The fully open petals are white, in contrast to the light yellow tones of the buds, the inner petals, and the dense, darker yellow tassels of stamens. This upright, broad bushy rose can be used in a mixed border with perennials in the same way as a bedding rose, and it will offer the advantage of long-lasting structure combined with a shade that harmonizes with all other colors in the planted bed. Four roses per square yard (square meter) will suffice if using for mass planting.

**FLOWERING:** Continuous; semi-double; Ø 1½–2 in. (4–5 cm.); white with creamy-white center; sweet scent

**GROWTH:** 20–24 in. (50–60 cm.) high; upright; broad and bushy

**FEATURES:** Heat and rain tolerant; suitable for container growing; attractive to bees; hardy

**PLANTING:** For flowerbeds, borders, and hedges; as specimens, in groups, and mass planting

**INTRODUCED:** Kordes, 1985, Germany

# 'THE FAIRY'

POLYANTHA / Synonyms: 'Fairy', 'Feerie', 'Féérie'

**FLOWERING:** Continuous; fully double; Ø ½–1½ in. (1–4 cm.); light pink
**GROWTH:** 20–24 in. (50–60 cm.) high; broad and bushy; densely branched
**FEATURES:** Heat, rain, and partial shade tolerant; suitable for pots; hardy
**PLANTING:** For borders, flowerbeds, and banks; attractive as quarter standard, half standard, standard, and weeping standard
**INTRODUCED:** Bentall, 1932, Great Britain

'The Fairy' is the "old favorite" among small shrub roses, and still as popular as ever—especially when trained as a standard. This delicate rose is a late bloomer—it does not open until July, but thereafter its small, dense clusters of emerging blooms begin to burst into flower in riotous profusion that is repeated from the end of August through well into fall. As the outer shoots of 'The Fairy' arch over, it is suitable for slopes and embankments, but also for planting against low walls to cover up the base. It is a lovely sight planted as edging on a patio to landscape the areas between seating and flowerbeds. In addition, when trained as a standard, it is able to bring a glorious element of height to formal bedding areas with its clouds of pink blooms spreading out above the plants.

◄ 'Simply' is an attractive, arching shrub rose that has small pink blooms of 1½ in. (4 cm.) in diameter. This very healthy, ADR-rated variety grows up to just over 3 ft. (1 m.) high and is suitable for plantings on banks and as hedging. Plant about four roses per square yard (square meter).

# 'SCHÖNE DORTMUNDERIN®'

Synonyms: 'Kleine Dortmunderin', 'Schöne Dortmunderin' / FLORIBUNDA

'Schone Dortmunderin®' blooms profusely in large clusters up to late fall. What is more the blooms look eye-catching from a distance as well as close up. The medium pink petals fade to translucent pink at the edges, so that every now and then they almost appear to be mixed with white. This play of colors and the lightly cupped bloom form, which also adds to the color effect, make them appear delicate and, at the same time, fresh and vibrant. Its compact, bushy growth habit, rather like a bedding rose, makes it suitable for edging along pathways, for planting in mixed beds or for landscaping a summer-house or pavilion. If planning to plant this healthy rose en masse, use four plants per square yard (square meter).

**FLOWERING:** Continuous bloomer; semi-double; Ø 1½ in. (4 cm.); pink

**GROWTH:** 24–28 in. (60–70 cm.) high; upright; bushy

**FEATURES:** ADR rating 1992; very healthy; heat, rain, and partial shade tolerant; attractive half standard or standard; hardy

**PLANTING:** For flowerbeds, borders, hedges, banks, and woodland edging; singly, in groups, or mass planting

**INTRODUCED:** Noack, 1991, Germany

# 'SWEET HAZE®'
## SMALL SHRUB ROSE

**FLOWERING:** Continuous bloomer; single; Ø 2–3 in. (5–7 cm.); pink; sweet fragrance

**GROWTH:** 20–28 in. (50–70 cm.) high; upright; very broad and bushy

**FEATURES:** ADR rating 2004; very healthy beginner's rose; heat and rain tolerant; suitable for container growing; hardy

**PLANTING:** For flowerbeds, borders, and hedges; as specimens, in groups or mass planting

**INTRODUCED:** Tantau, 2003, Germany

This multi-award-winning rose has been a great success for its breeder, Tantau. It is the most charming representative of the new generation of ground-cover roses. From June onward, its delicate pink, single blooms open and flower so profusely as to cover the broad, bushy shrub completely. At the same time they offer a delightful display of different shades of pink, depending on their age. After fading the petals fall off completely, so that the rose always looks "clean" and can continue to produce new blooms. To the breeder's delight 'Sweet Haze®' has also proved to be exceedingly healthy and is actually able to suppress weeds when used in mass plantings of three per square yard (square meter).

# 'PALMENGARTEN FRANKFURT®'

Synonyms: 'Beauce', 'Our Rosy Carpet' / SMALL SHRUB ROSE

'Palmengarten Frankfurt®' is a richly blooming variety. Its crimson-pink hues make a perfect foil for the glossy foliage. The medium-sized blooms emerge from June onward in huge open clusters on the spreading, bushy, arching shrub. This rose is a perfect example of a magnificent ground-cover plant, being robust and extremely healthy, even performing well in less favorable locations. It looks attractive when planted as a specimen in a herbaceous perennial bed or in groups against walls, beneath trees, and in hedges. It makes a fine low hedge, is suitable for containers or to bring a splash of color to buildings. The massed effect of carmine-pink 'Palmengarten Frankfurt®' can be used successfully to cover a terrace bank, a small slope, or even as edging along pathways. For this, four plants per square yard (square meter) will suffice.

▶ 'Heidetraum' (synonyms: 'Flower Carpet', 'Emera') is another bright, even dazzling carmine-pink rose. This world-renowned, healthy, top-quality, ADR-rated rose does not open till July, but then blooms tirelessly, whether as a 28-in. (70-cm.) high shrub or as a standard.

**FLOWERING:** Continuous bloomer; loosely double; Ø 1½–2 in. (4–5 cm.); deep carmine pink; no scent
**GROWTH:** 24–39 in. (60–100 cm.) high; bushy
**FEATURES:** ADR rating 1992; robust beginner's rose; heat, rain, and partial shade tolerant; for containers; as a standard; hardy
**PLANTING:** For borders, flowerbeds, and hedges; as ground cover; singly, in groups, or mass planting
**INTRODUCED:** Kordes, 1988, Germany

# 'KNIRPS®'

SMALL SHRUB ROSE / Synonyms: 'County of Hampshire', 'Little Cap'

Continuous abundant blooming and low-lying, compact growth make 'Knirps®' ideal ground cover for small yards, where it will stage a long-lasting blooming display. Of course, it is capable of covering large areas, but will also make lovely, decorative edging to pathways, where its carmine-pink blooms will give a scintillating, continuous show of color. What is more, the blooms alternate between darker and lighter nuances as they lighten with age. This exceptionally healthy rose can be used to great effect to landscape different areas of the yard, such as between terrace and yard, pathway and lawn, between walls/hedges and pathways/lawns, as well as between the house, summer-house, or pavilion and yard. Plant 16 in. (40 cm.) apart or five per square yard (square meter).

**FLOWERING:** Continuous bloomer; fully double; Ø 1¼ in. (3 cm.); deep pink; no scent

**GROWTH:** 12 in. (30 cm.) high; compact; low-lying; twice as broad as it is high

**FEATURES:** ADR rating 2004; heat tolerant; for pots, troughs, and boxes; attractive as half standard and standard; hardy

**PLANTING:** For flowerbeds, borders, and banks; singly, in groups, or mass planting

**INTRODUCED:** Kordes, 1997, Germany

# 'SCARLET MEIDILAND'

SMALL SHRUB ROSE / Synonym: 'Scarlet Meillandecor'

**FLOWERING:** Repeat bloomer; double; Ø ¾–1½ in. (2–3 cm.); hot dark red; no scent

**GROWTH:** 20–24 in. (50–60 cm.) high; arching; long shoots

**FEATURES:** Heat and rain tolerant; excellent leaf health; suitable for container growing; makes an attractive half standard, standard, and weeping standard; hardy

**PLANTING:** For flowerbeds, borders, banks, and hedges; as specimens, in groups or mass planting

**INTRODUCED:** Meilland, 1987, France

Those who offer beautiful 'Scarlet Meidiland' a home in their yard must be prepared to offer it what it really longs for—a location in full sun so that its blooms may open enough to achieve their full potential. Of course, this should not be in close proximity to a dazzling white wall in glaring sunlight, but rather in an airy, sunny location. Nothing—not direct sunlight or heat or rain—can diminish the intense scarlet red of this variety. Its dazzling effect from a distance is intensified due to the tiny blooms being borne in huge clusters of as many as 25 each. 'Scarlet Meidiland' does not begin to bloom until July. As its blooms emerge at the end of long stems, it is also eminently suitable for cutting and makes a decorative display in a vase.

# 'ROTE WOGE®'

SHRUB ROSE

'Rote Woge®' is classified as a shrub rose in some rose catalogs, as it is just as convincing as a richly blooming shrub as it is as taller ground cover in a massed planting. This very robust rose often begins to open its medium-sized blooms at the end of May, pauses a little in August, and then begins to bloom afresh from September onward almost as abundantly as it did before. If it is to be planted as a loosely growing hedge, it is best planted 20–24 in. (50–60 cm.) apart. If plants are needed to landscape a slope, say on a banked terrace, use three to four roses per square yard (square meter). The dark green foliage has proved to be extraordinarily resistant to mildew and black spot, so wherever it is planted—in private yards or in public green spaces—it hardly ever succumbs to disease.

▶ 'Heidefeuer' (synonym: 'Red Flower Carpet') has dazzling red blooms, and at 20 to 24 in. (50 to 60 cm.) high with compact, upright growth habit, it may be used as a bedding rose. In fall the rosehips give a delightful display.

**FLOWERING:** Twice-blooming; double; Ø 2½ in. (6 cm.); dark red; no scent

**GROWTH:** 32–47 in. (80–120 cm.) high; strong; upright; arching

**FEATURES:** ADR rating 1992; heat, rain, and partial shade tolerant; hardy

**PLANTING:** For flowerbeds, borders, and hedges; singly, in groups, or mass planting

**INTRODUCED:** Meilland, 1992, France

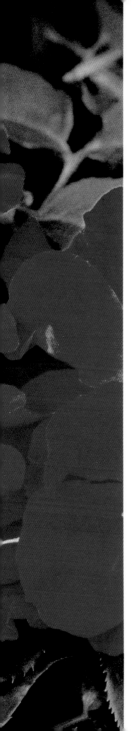

# 'ROYAL BASSINO®'

SMALL SHRUB ROSE / Synonym: 'Country Prince'

It is no coincidence that this rose has "royal" in its name. It really makes an impression with its dazzling crimson blooms, which are relatively large for a small shrub rose and have wavy petals with a dished form. At the center of the bloom, looking rather like an eye, is a dense cluster of bright yellow stamens. The blooms are borne in large, round clusters at the end of broad and numerous lightly arching shoots, so that the shiny, dark green foliage seems to almost completely disappear beneath them. This concentration of blooms intensifies the color display: the rose really catches the eye from afar. If this effect is required, use three to four roses per square yard (square meter) for a mass planting.

**FLOWERING:** Repeat bloomer; semi-double; Ø 2–2½ in. (5–6 cm.); dazzling crimson; no scent
**GROWTH:** 20–24 in. (50–60 cm.) high; semi-upright; broad and bushy
**FEATURES:** Heat and rain tolerant; suitable for container growing; hardy
**PLANTING:** For flowerbeds, borders, and slopes; singly, in groups, and mass planting
**INTRODUCED:** Kordes, 1991, Germany

▼ 'Red Ribbons' (synonyms: 'Mainaufeuer®', 'Fiery Sensation', 'Island Fire', 'Chilterns', 'Canterbury') is the same height as 'Royal Bassino®'; however, it has a somewhat fuller-shaped bloom that flowers continuously.

# 'LOREDO'

SMALL SHRUB ROSE / Synonyms: 'Flower Carpet Gold', 'Suneva'

**FLOWERING:** Repeat bloomer; semi-double; Ø 2–2½ in. (5–6 cm.); bright yellow; lightly scented

**GROWTH:** 24–28 in. (60–70 cm.) high; very upright; bushy

**FEATURES:** ADR rating 2001; heat and rain tolerant; stable color; very healthy and disease-resistant; hardy

**PLANTING:** For flowerbeds and borders; singly, in groups, or mass planting

**INTRODUCED:** Noack, 2002, Germany

Breeding landscape roses in yellow and orange has been unsuccessful until recently. The problem lay in trying to eliminate the genetic frailty and susceptibility to frost of the yellow varieties, as ground-cover roses should not only bloom profusely, but also demonstrate robustness, ease of maintenance, and good health. All these characteristics are to be found in 'Loredo'. If it is used for landscaping, it will produce large masses of yellow, but careful thought should be given to color combinations. It always looks more attractive not to have one mass of color clashing with another; it is better to create colorful accents by using different-sized splashes of color. These shades look very pretty when planted together: silver, gray, blue, violet blue, apricot orange, copper, and yellowish green.

# 'SUNNY ROSE®'

SMALL SHRUB ROSE

The small, semi-double blooms of 'Sunny Rose®' have such a light and hazy effect that they appear to be suffused with light. And in fact the light does reflect in the creamy-yellow, delicate petals that surround masses of very bright shiny stamens. The blooms stand out like glittering jewels, especially against the background of the dark green, very glossy foliage. This flat-growing rose is very effective as a foreground planting in beds and borders, where its pastel shade will combine excellently with many other colors and plants. For those seeking to plant bedding with finely graduated color tones, selecting a pale yellow shade rather than a deeper yellow will make the task a lot easier. This rule applies to all planting, not just roses.

**FLOWERING:** Repeat bloomer; semi-double; Ø 1¼ in. (3 cm.); pale yellow; no scent

**GROWTH:** 12 in. (30 cm.) high; broad to low-lying

**FEATURES:** ADR rating 2004; rain tolerant; very healthy; attracts bees; makes a lovely standard or half-standard rose; hardy

**PLANTING:** For flowerbeds, borders, and banks; singly, in groups, or mass planting

**INTRODUCED:** Kordes, 2001, Germany

▶ 'Celina' (synonym: 'Flower Carpet Yellow') is also a delightful rose. It has cream-yellow blooms that flower abundantly and is healthy. This 24-in. (60-cm.) high, broad and bushy Noack breed achieved an ADR rating for these qualities in 1999.

# 'CONCERTO '94®'

SMALL SHRUB ROSE, ROMANTICA ROSE / Synonym: 'Concerto'

**FLOWERING:** Repeat bloomer; fully double; Ø 2–2½ in. (5–6 cm.); yellow-pink
**GROWTH:** 24–32 in. (60–80 cm.) high; upright; broad and bushy
**FEATURES:** Heat tolerant; very resistant to rain; suitable for container growing; attractive standard rose; hardy
**PLANTING:** For flowerbeds, borders, and hedges; as specimen roses, in groups or mass planting
**INTRODUCED:** Meilland, 1994, France

'Concerto '94®' has successfully combined two current "rose trends" in one rose and is also suitable for planting as ground cover. First is the preference for soft yellow and salmon-pink tones of varying intensity, and second is the fondness for "old-fashioned" bloom forms. As 'Concerto '94®' unites both these trends, it has been included in the Romantica rose series by its breeder, Meilland. Due to its resistance to both mildew and black spot, it is suitable for use as a bedding rose in garden design and will harmonize beautifully with blue companions. Its vigor and broad, bushy growth habit also make it eminently suitable for massed landscaping. Plant three to four roses per square yard (square meter).

◀ Amber-colored 'Taos' (synonyms: 'Amber Cover®', 'Towne & Country®', 'Poulbambe') has a similar growth habit to 'Concerto '94®'—upright and broad and it, too, is suitable for container growing. Its round, dished blooms also live up to the ideal of an "old-fashioned" rose.

# 'CUBANA®'
SMALL SHRUB ROSE

'Cubana®' also reflects the preference for "old-fashioned" blooms and colors. Its dainty ruffled petals open a pretty apricot and then the blooms begin to turn an intense pink from the edges and finally fade to creamy white. They are borne on their stems in large dense clusters, which gives them the air of colorful, gay abandon. 'Cubana®' lends itself to use in mixed borders in the same way as a bedding rose, and looks terrific with companions that pick up its range of colors, whereas blue or purple plants will make a more vibrant contrast. For a colorful visual display, plant en masse with four roses per square yard (square meter); try landscaping the bed with ornamental round trimmed box or small, neatly shaped conifers.

▶ 'Sedana', from Noack's Flower Carpet range, also gives an original display of color. Its pretty, semi-double blooms open apricot, turn to delicate pink and then to creamy orange on fading.

**FLOWERING:** Continuous bloomer; semi-double; Ø 2 in. (5 cm.); apricot turning to pink then cream-white; no scent
**GROWTH:** 20 in. (50 cm.) high and 20 in. (50 cm.) wide; bushy; lightly arching
**FEATURES:** Heat and rain tolerant; suitable for container growing; good resistance to mildew; hardy
**PLANTING:** For flowerbeds and borders; singly, in groups, or mass planting
**INTRODUCED:** Kordes, 2001, Germany

# MINIATURE ROSES

# MINIATURE ROSES

## Miniature and/or patio roses?

There is still no definite consensus or ruling on what constitutes a miniature or a patio rose. Whereas in the United States the terms patio rose and miniature rose are almost

There are many varieties of multicolored miniature roses or, like 'Mandarin', roses that put on a delightful play of colors right up to fading.

interchangeable, elsewhere the term miniature generally refers to roses that should grow no higher than 12 in. (30 cm.) and bear especially small blooms, and the term patio rose to those roses that grow up to 20 in. (50 cm.) high and have normal-sized blooms. Some catalogs use the term "miniature roses"; others predominantly "patio roses." There is no need to be put off buying the product, but just be mindful of the instructions given for each particular rose. In the following chapter the term "miniature rose" will be employed as an over-arching expression for all small roses, and the growing height given will be the key to classifying whether the rose is a miniature or patio variety.

Nor should the following roses be confused with so-called "Mother's Day" roses, or miniature roses for indoors or greenhouse, as these are almost always grown from cuttings and can be cultivated in small pots. The roses illustrated in this chapter are grafted bushes that put on good growth due to the growing strength of the rootstock. With good protection they should be able to survive the winter in containers. The container should be at least 14 in. (35 cm.) deep, as the union should be embedded 2 in. (5 cm.) below the surface of the soil.

**PAGES 216–17**
Miniature roses can bring to life small sunny niches and corners on a balcony or terrace. Here they make a delightful group of small bushes of varying heights—as quarter standards and half standards.

**WATERING TIP**
Fungal spores can attack roses in no time. To prevent this happening, do not water above the foliage of miniature roses and do not use too harsh a spray setting on the hose so that soil does not mix with the water and reach the leaves.

**Can miniature roses be grown in beds or only in containers?**

The history of miniature roses began with 'Rouletii', a deep pink rose that was discovered in around 1918 growing

Transitions are smooth in the rose world. The enchanting, white-bloomed 'Swany' will flourish as a 16-in. (40-cm.) high, low-lying small shrub rose, as a patio rose in a pot or (as pictured here) trained as a standard rose.

in a pot on a windowsill in Switzerland. This rose also became famous under the name 'Pompon de Paris' as the smallest rose in the world. This resulted in a frenzy of miniature rose breeding in the United States. Until a few years ago it was recommended that these roses should not be used as bedding plants but should be grown only in containers. This was due to the fact that if they are planted in a bed, they fall prey to black spot and other fungal diseases very rapidly as their low-lying foliage is usually sitting directly on the soil and it can only dry off very slowly. Since then, some extremely robust and healthy varieties have been bred that even lend themselves to being used as mass plantings in small yards. Another problem when planting them in beds are vigorous perennials and trees, which will compete with these delicate roses for light, air, and nutrients. One solution might be to plant the rose into a pot directly into the bed. Miniature roses, therefore, are best planted in containers: the risk of disease is significantly less in this case because the roses are further from the soil. Varieties that are grafted onto quarter or half standards are particularly healthy, as the risk of water (which will be contaminated by spores from the soil) reaching the leaves is lower.

## The right spot for miniature roses

Roses in pots make it possible, even where the soil is poor, to avoid having to do without the "romance of the rose." Balconies and patios, a paved seating area, a sunny front doorway, a sunny rock garden, a wall, steps in the sun, or even a grave—the possibilities for siting miniature roses and their standards are virtually endless, providing they have an airy and humid spot. However, against an outside wall on a south-facing terrace, for example—if the wall and surface of the patio have a tendency to trap and radiate the heat and dry out the air—they will be stunted and sick.

# 'ZWERGKÖNIG '78®'

MINIATURE ROSE / Synonym: 'Dwarf King '78'

**FLOWERING:** In flushes; loosely double; Ø 2 in. (5 cm.); velvety crimson; no scent

**GROWTH:** 16–20 in. (40–50 cm.) high; bushy

**FEATURES:** Rain resistant; partial shade tolerant; very hardy

**PLANTING:** For container growing and as a bedding rose; lovely half standard

**INTRODUCED:** Kordes, 1978, Germany

This very largely brilliant red classic among miniature roses is just as suitable for tubs and troughs as it is for low hedges and edging to beds or borders. The crimson blooms open in June from pointed, conical buds. When fully opened the petals stand out in stark contrast to the masses of golden-yellow stamens. The blooms grow in clusters, stand up well in rain, and emerge up until fall. For larger pots, plant two to three roses for a really exuberant display. Plant 12 in. (30 cm.) apart in beds, and for mass planting seven to eight plants per square yard (square meter) are needed. As this variety is susceptible to black spot and mildew, preventative spraying with fungicide is recommended when the leaves appear.

◀ 'Red Det '80', the scarlet dwarf rose bred by Cocker, United States, not only differs from 'Zwergkönig' in color, but also has hybrid Tea-like blooms and is smaller by 8–16 in. (20–40 cm.).

# 'MEDLEY RED'
## MINIATURE ROSE

'Medley Red' has a cumulative effect: it is both a bedding rose and miniature rose. It will be prized as low edging in a flowerbed, its blooms providing long-lasting color. As a grave planting in a sunny position it will symbolize loving memories. However, in containers it is particularly versatile. It may fulfill the function of combining height with a colorful accent by dominating a crossing of pathways when used as a standard rose; it may be used as a duo either side of a seating area or a path, or as an eye-catching feature in a flowerbed. This rose can also be displayed in a bowl on a pedestal or column to give the effect of height. Spaces in beds can also be filled decoratively by potted roses, as can almost any sunny spot on the balcony or patio.

▶ Scarlet-red 'Top Marks' (synonym: 'Fryministar') is brighter even than 'Medley Red'. This hardy, broad but compact miniature rose, bred by Fryer, grows to 8–16 in. (20–40 cm.) high and produces round, dish-shaped blooms.

**FLOWERING:** Continuous bloomer; semi-double; Ø 2–2¼ in. (5–6 cm.); crimson; no scent

**GROWTH:** 12–16 in. (30–40 cm.) high; bushy

**FEATURES:** Good in rain; vigorous foliage; requires protection in winter

**PLANTING:** For container growing and as a bedding rose; for small yard and grave planting; attractive as a quarter standard, half standard, and standard

**INTRODUCED:** Noack, 2002–2003, Germany

# 'AMULETT®'
MINIATURE ROSE

**FLOWERING:** Continuous bloomer; fully double; Ø 1¼–1½ in. (3–4 cm.); deep pink; no scent
**GROWTH:** 16–24 in. (40–60 cm.) high; broad and bushy; lightly arching
**FEATURES:** Vigorous; moderate rain resistance; heat tolerant; requires protection in winter
**PLANTING:** For container growing and as a bedding rose; lovely half standard or standard rose
**INTRODUCED:** Tantau, 1991, Germany

'Amulett®' turns out to be a tireless and long-lasting bloomer, whether in pots, troughs, or in beds. In June its round rosette-shaped blooms open from globular red buds. The petals are arranged so exactly one on top of the other like roof tiles that they look rather like pompon dahlias. Their initial deep pink hue takes on a silvery sheen on fading. As the foliage of this rose is exceptionally resistant to mildew and has moderate resistance to black spot, it is suitable for planting in the yard, so long as it is sprayed to prevent disease occurring. It looks charming as edging at the front of a mixed border around the patio. But it can also be used in containers as edging for beds, pathways, or on larger graves, where it will provide color throughout the summer.

# 'PEPITA®'
## MINIATURE ROSE

'Pepita®' is characterized by its breeder as being one of the most delicate and appealing miniature roses of 'The Fairy' type. The rose unfolds its fully double blooms in June, which are borne in dense, gossamer-fine clusters of six to eight that gradually fade to a silvery sheen. They bloom abundantly in flushes, sitting atop very glossy foliage that is remarkably resistant to mildew and black spot. If 'Pepita®' is to be used as a small standard with a planting beneath, use companions that also have small blooms, such as white sweet alyssum (*Lobularia maritima*), so that they are not in competition with one another. Also, choose a larger container, so that the rose's roots will not be affected when planting the summer flowers.

▶ 'Sugar Baby®' (synonym: 'Tanabagus'), a similar pink shade, has won many international awards. This compact variety by Tantau, with charming hybrid Tea-type mini-blooms, also comes in half-standard or full-standard forms.

**FLOWERING:** Repeat bloomer; fully double; Ø 1¼ in. (3 cm.); deep pink; no scent

**GROWTH:** 12–20 in. (30–50 cm.) high; broad and bushy; compact

**FEATURES:** ADR rating 2004; easy-to-maintain beginner's rose with healthy leaves; good in rain; heat tolerant

**PLANTING:** For container growing, as bedding rose, or delicate ground cover; attractive as half standard and full standard

**INTRODUCED:** Kordes, 2004, Germany

# 'CORAL PAGODE®'
MINIATURE ROSE

**FLOWERING:** Repeat bloomer; double; Ø 1½–2 in. (4–5 cm.); salmon to delicate pink; lightly scented
**GROWTH:** 16–20 in. (40–50 cm.) high; many shoots; arching
**FEATURES:** Vigorous and rain resistant; heat and partial shade tolerant; requires protection in winter
**PLANTING:** For hanging pots, baskets, and bowls on columns, pedestals, and walls
**INTRODUCED:** Poulsen, 2000, Denmark

The miniature roses in the PAGODE® collection provide decorative floral interest to architectural settings such as patios, balconies, or pavilions. They are notable for their abundance of small double blooms that hang in clusters at the end of numerous short stems. This growth habit makes them ideal for hanging flowerpots, baskets, or containers placed up high, from where the shoots will be able to trail down romantically. As well as 'Coral Pagode®' Poulgo003®, with its hot pink nuances, there are varieties in five further colors: 'Pink Pagode' is light pink, 'Rosy Pagode' a delicate pink, 'Red Pagode' has crimson blooms, 'White Pagode' is pure snow-white, and 'Yellow Pagode' has small yellow cascades of blooms.

◀ 'Biedermeier®' is a completely different type of romantic miniature rose. It features extremely delicate cherry-red, greenish-white, spherical-shaped blooms. The large-flowered Tantau variety is fabulous in standard form and it is also very frost hardy.

# 'LUPO®'
## MINIATURE ROSE

'Lupo®' embodies the ever-growing popularity of simple blooms mixed with "wild rose" charm. Its vibrant shade of carmine red tinged with mauve is not, however, characteristic of a wild rose at all. Its effect from afar is brilliant without being garish. The color combines wonderfully with carmine red, pink, blue, blue mauve, and silver shades; even cool pastel yellow can go well with it. This little gem looks delightful in pots, or as edging for a bed. As 'Lupo®' has enormous resistance to mildew and black spot, it is eminently suitable for planting on small slopes and banks to create an endless sea of flowers. For that, six plants per square yard (square meter) is needed.

**FLOWERING:** Repeat bloomer; single; ∅ 1¼ in. (3 cm.); dark mauve to carmine red; no scent

**GROWTH:** 12–16 in. (30–40 cm.) high; dense; bushy

**FEATURES:** Robust; good in rain; heat and partial shade tolerant; attractive rosehips; hardy

**PLANTING:** For container growing, bedding rose, or small ground cover; enchanting full standard

**INTRODUCED:** Kordes, 2006, Germany

▶ 'Zwergkönigin '82®' has medium pink blooms that stand out well against the foliage and change color in the light. This semi-double, classic miniature rose has a light fragrance, stands up very well in rain and together with 'Zwergkönig '78®' makes a pretty combination.

# 'SGANARELLE'
MINIATURE ROSE

**FLOWERING:** Repeat bloomer; fully double; Ø 1½–2 in. (4–5 cm.); yellow, orange, and red; no scent

**GROWTH:** 16 in. (40 cm.) high; broad and bushy

**FEATURES:** For sun or partial shade; requires protection in winter

**PLANTING:** For troughs and pots; an enchanting small standard

**INTRODUCED:** Delbard, 2005, France

The appeal of the striped Painters' roses collection (see p. 133) has now been recreated in a smaller format by Delbard's 'Sganarelle'. This miniature Painters' Rose grows to around 16 in. (40 cm.) high and should preferably be planted as a trio in containers such as pots, boxes, troughs, etc. at least 16 in. (40 cm.) deep. As well as the potpourri of colors displayed by 'Sganarelle', there is another miniature Painters' rose called 'Papillon' that has wine-red stripes on a white-pink background. These roses are not noted for their hardiness; therefore they should be well protected in harsher zones or, even better, they may be overwintered in their containers in a glasshouse or a garage. However, do not let them dry out.

# 'BLUENETTE®'

Synonyms: 'Blue Peter', 'Azulabria' / MINIATURE ROSE

Exotic rose enthusiasts often have a weakness for so-called "blue" roses too. This is a romantic notion, a symbol of longing, and still unattainable. There are some miniature roses, however, that tend toward cool, bluish-mauve tones. 'Bluenette®' is probably the best known of these roses. Its carmine red with mauve blooms unfold from slender, elegant hybrid Tea-type buds. When fully open, dense tufts of yellow stamens are visible. The shades of color will fade with time, but this will happen more rapidly if the rose is in full sun and especially if exposed to the glare of the midday sun. It makes a really striking edging to a bed. Whether it is planted in pots or in flowerbeds, it will require protection in winter.

▶ The 12-in. (30-cm.) high patio rose, 'Baby Faurax', bred in 1924 by Leonard Lille, is also a "blue-blooded" rose. Give it a location that protects it from the midday sun, so that the fresh lilac tones do not fade to gray too soon.

**FLOWERING:** Repeat bloomer; semi double; Ø 1–1¼ in. (2½–3 cm.); lilac; no scent

**GROWTH:** 8–16 in. (20–40 cm.) high; broad and bushy; branched

**FEATURES:** Relatively rain resistant; tolerates partial shade; requires protection in winter

**PLANTING:** For pots, boxes, troughs, and also beds

**INTRODUCED:** De Ruiter, 1983, Holland

# 'WHITE PET'

ROSE / Synonyms: 'Little White Pet', 'Little Pet', 'Little Dot',
'Belle de Teheran', 'Belle of Tehran'

Even before the beginning of official miniature rose breeding,
there were isolated cases of especially small-growing roses,
which were without exception accidental gifts of nature. This
was the case with the variety formerly known as 'Little White
Pet', a sport of the climber 'Félicité et Perpétue'. From June
onward, deep pink buds unfold into a sea of delicate blooms.
Initially they are cupped with the outer petals tinged pink,
but when the blooms have fully opened to perfect rosette
form, they are pure white, making a rich contrast with the
dark green foliage. A robust continuous bloomer, it is suitable
for bedding as well as pots. Best of all, in standard form, it
makes an outstanding feature—its abundant blooms floating
like clouds above the flowerbed.

**FLOWERING:** Continuous bloomer; densely double; Ø 1½ in. (4 cm.);
pure white with delicate pink; delicate fragrance
**GROWTH:** 12–20 in. (30–50 cm.) high; broad and bushy; vigorous with
plentiful shoots
**FEATURES:** Robust and rain resistant; heat and partial rain tolerant; hardy
**PLANTING:** Best suited to containers, as bedding rose, or small ground
cover; enchanting in standard form
**INTRODUCED:** Henderson, 1879, USA

▼ Due to its extremely healthy foliage, the miniature rose
'Sonnenröschen®' (Kordes, 2005, ADR rating 2003) not only
thrives in containers, but also flourishes magnificently as a
bedding rose. It grows 12 in. (30 cm.) high and blooms tirelessly.

# 'SONNENKIND'

MINIATURE ROSE / Synonyms: 'Perestroika', 'Golden Fire'

**FLOWERING:** Repeat bloomer; double; Ø 1¼ in. (3 cm.); golden yellow; no scent
**GROWTH:** Up to 14 in. (35 cm.) high; upright; broad and bushy; compact
**FEATURES:** Robust and rain resistant; heat and partial shade tolerant; hardy
**PLANTING:** For pots and boxes; as bedding or small ground cover; for rock gardens; attractive standard
**INTRODUCED:** Kordes, 1986, Germany

'Sonnenkind' is another of those miniature roses that is able to perform two tasks at the same time because it not only thrives in containers but it is also rarely prey to fungal diseases if used in bedding. So this charming little plant can spread its sunny rays of color on a balcony, a terrace, or in the yard. It almost appears as if the bloom form of 'Sonnenkind' wishes to emphasize its empathy with the sun—as soon as the bloom unfurls, almost all the outer petals reflex, so that pointed petals encircle the center making it look as if it is surrounded by the sun's rays. Dark green, glossy foliage sets this shape off a treat. For a colorful accent in the yard, plant 'Sonnenkind' as a half standard in a pot with an underplanting of white sweet alyssum (*Lobularia maritima*), light blue trailing Calibrachoa 'Celebration Silver Blue' or dark blue lobelia (Lobelia 'Hot-Blue').

# 'LAURA FORD'

Synonyms: 'King Tut', 'Normandie' / CLIMBING MINIATURE

Lovely 'Laura Ford' is one of the climbing miniatures that Chris Warner has introduced. Its small hybrid Tea-type blooms and delicate foliage actually resemble a miniature rose. This repeat flowering climber, however, will grow up to 8 ft. (2.5 m.) high, and in warm zones even higher—ideal for trailing up columns or trellises. When the yellow flowers open in June from pink tinged buds, there is often still a trace of pink on the petal edges. This will disappear with time. However, in fall, when the blooms start to take on deep pink hues, these "rosy cheeks" are a phenomenon specific to some varieties of yellow roses, which react to the first cold snaps in this way.

▶ 'Guletta' (synonyms: 'Golden Penny', 'Goldpenny', 'Tapis Jaune', 'Rugul'), bred by De Ruiter, has citrus yellow, rain-resistant hybrid Tea-type blooms in miniature and does well in rock gardens and grave plantings in partial shade.

**FLOWERING:** Continuous bloomer; semi-double; Ø 1½–2 in. (4–5 cm.); yellow with amber heart; fruity scent

**GROWTH:** Climbs up to 8 ft. (2.5 m.)

**FEATURES:** Heat tolerant; requires protection in winter

**PLANTING:** For arches, obelisks, pyramids, trellises, and other climbing supports, either in pots or as bedding

**INTRODUCED:** Warner, 1989, Great Britain

# 'MANDARIN®'
MINIATURE ROSE

**FLOWERING:** Continuous bloomer; fully double; Ø 1½ in. (4 cm.); salmon pink, orange, and yellow; no scent

**GROWTH:** Up to 10 in. (25 cm.) high; broad and bushy; compact

**FEATURES:** Holds up well in rain; heat tolerant; susceptible to black spot; requires protection in winter

**PLANTING:** Suitable for container growing and as a bedding rose; attractive half standard

**INTRODUCED:** Kordes, 1987, Germany

From June onward, 'Mandarin®' makes a glorious colorful flowering spectacle when its blooms unfurl above small, glossy, medium green leaves. The blooms readily change their color—initially they are pink orange with golden centers, whereas later hot sunny yellow dominates as the mandarin and rose tints lose their brightness to fade to pastel shades. Due to its susceptibility to black spot, 'Mandarin®' will serve best if it is planted in a container. It may then be used to fill in any spaces in bedding with intense color, enhance a patio with its colorful display, or be trained as a half standard to provide an attractive element of height to a potted planting.

# 'COCO®'
## MINIATURE ROSE

The pink tones of the lightly ruffled petals make 'Coco®' appear as if bathed in the light of the setting sun. The hot salmon pink of the petals is a perfect match for the masses of yellow stamens that completely fill the heart. Thanks to its resistance to black spot and mildew, it can be used at the front of bedding or for grave planting. As the spores of black spot spread out over the surface of the soil and the foliage of miniature roses lies very close to the ground, these roses are particularly susceptible; therefore only the most robust varieties should be planted direct into the earth. If they are attacked by disease, leaves should be removed immediately and the rose should be sprayed with fungicide.

**FLOWERING:** Continuous bloomer; single; Ø 1¼ in. (3 cm.); salmon orange to salmon pink; no scent

**GROWTH:** Up to 16 in. (40 cm.) high; bushy; plentiful shoots; very compact

**FEATURES:** Robust; rain resistant; heat and partial shade tolerant; good resistance to black spot and mildew; hardy

**PLANTING:** For containers, beds, and grave planting

**INTRODUCED:** Kordes, 2006, Germany

# 'FAVOURITE™' HIT®

MINIATURE ROSE / Synonyms: 'Good Wishes', 'Favourite®', 'Poululv®'

**FLOWERING:** Repeat bloomer; double; Ø 2–2½ in. (5–6 cm.); apricot with yellow and pink nuances; no scent

**GROWTH:** 16–24 in. (40–60 cm.) high; bushy; compact

**FEATURES:** Robust and very disease resistant; requires protection in winter

**PLANTING:** For container growing

**INTRODUCED:** Poulsen, 2002, Denmark

'Favourite™' Hit® Poululv® embodies in its shape and color all the attributes of an "old-fashioned," romantic miniature rose. The initially round, dish-shaped blooms open out slowly to reveal the stamens. In doing so they shimmer in tones of yellowish apricot, together with amber-yellow tawny shades. 'Favourite™' belongs to the PATIOHIT® collection by the Danish breeder Poulsen, who has created more than sixty varieties, in all colors, especially designed for container growing on patios. They have proved to be highly disease resistant. For those who desire an even smaller rose, these are to be found in Poulsen's PARADE® collection, which also offers a huge variety of roses up to 12 in. (30 cm.) in height in every rose color under the sun.

◀ 'Feminine™' Hit® (synonym: 'Retirement Wishes') is another fabulous PATIOHIT® rose in soft apricot tones. It looks extremely delicate, has tiny flowers, and stands no more than 16 in. (40 cm.) high.

# 'SWEET DREAM'

Synonyms: 'Sweet Dreams', 'Apricot Sweet Dream', 'Fryminicot' / ROSE

Patio rose 'Sweet Dream' is only 18 in. (45 cm.) high, with clusters of peach-colored blooms that flower continuously from June through fall. This rose may be small but it has achieved phenomenal success. It was not only awarded Rose of the Year in 1988 in Great Britain and the prestigious Award of Garden Merit by the Royal Horticultural Society, but with more than 4.5 million sales it is quite simply the best-selling British rose ever. And no wonder, it flourishes in pots just as well as it does planted in a bed. Its romantic, long-lasting blooms are delightful in containers, or it can be used as a small standard with an underplanting to set off porch, patio, or bare patches in bedding with colorful, long-lasting accents. It makes an attractive edging to the front of a bed and can be used to create a floriferous low hedge.

▶ 'Apricot Clementine®', a patio rose by Tantau, is equally resistant to disease and grows up to 22 in. (55 cm.) with long-lasting apricot blooms. It is also available as a half or full standard.

**FLOWERING:** Continuous bloomer; double; Ø 2½–3 in. (6–8 cm.); apricot; delicate fragrance

**GROWTH:** 18 in. (45 cm.) high; compact; bushy

**FEATURES:** Rose of the Year, 1988, UK; requires protection in winter

**PLANTING:** For container growing or as bedding rose; attractive quarter, half, or full standard

**INTRODUCED:** Fryer, 1988, Great Britain

# WILD ROSES

# WILD ROSES

## Wild roses—the potential of the varieties

Around 150 wild rose species have contributed to the almost 30,000 cultivated rose varieties that exist today. Wild roses are distinguished by single blooms of five petals

(except for *Rosa sericea*, which has four) and by decorative rosehips in fall. Their natural area of distribution is the northern hemisphere—they come from Europe, America, Asia, and the Middle East. Wild roses brought their genetic make-up and characteristics in quite different ways to countless varieties, resulting time and again in new breeds.

*Rosa foetida* 'Bicolor' has unusual orange-colored blooms. Its origins go back to the 16th century.

Wild roses existed even before people. Their path to domesticity began probably well over 5,000 years ago in the yards of China. Today, wild roses look at their best in wild gardens, cottage gardens, in large open spaces, or even managed nature reserves.

## European wild roses

These bloom just once per season and are generally frost hardy. The most important predecessors of shrub roses were: *Rosa canina*, the dog rose (p. 240), *Rosa glauca*, the red-leafed rose (p. 242), *Rosa rubiginosa*, eglantine or sweetbriar (p. 241), *Rosa villosa*, the apple rose, so-called after the shape of its soft-skinned rosehips, *Rosa pimpinellifolia*, the Burnet rose (p. 243), with its delicate foliage and black rosehips, *Rosa majalis* (p. 242), *Rosa pendulina*, whose variety 'Bourgogne' earns its place in the yard due to its strikingly attractive hips, and *Rosa gallica*, the French rose, which lends itself to hybridization and which is an ancestor of the beautiful Gallica roses, typified by their wonderful shades of pink and deep red. Important ancestors of the climbing roses are *Rosa arvensis*, the field rose, and *Rosa sempervirens*, the evergreen and frost-tender rose that is native to the Mediterranean.

**PAGES 236–7**

From left to right: White Burnet rose (*Rosa pimpinellifolia/spinosissima*), above, *Rosa ultramontane*; beside it, deep pink *Rosa nutkana* 'Cantab'; below, the particularly large and beautiful deep pink bloom of *Rosa oxyodon*; on the far right of the picture the delicate bloom of *Rosa canina* in whitish, mother-of-pearl hue.

## Wild roses from the Middle East

Wild roses that come from Asia Minor are

The blackish-red hips of *Rosa spinosissima* are flatter and rounder than the "little apples" of *Rosa rugosa* (above left). The green chestnut shape of *Rosa roxburghii* (above the bottle-shaped hips of *Rosa sweginzowii* 'Macrocarpa') is unusual.

important in the development of cultivated varieties, especially the yellow roses, as they introduced the strong yellow color into modern varieties. Among them are: *Rosa foetida*, Austrian briar, *Rosa foetida* 'Bicolor' (p. 244), the Capucine briar; and also the already hybridized, double, yellow roses, *Rosa hemisphaerica* and *Rosa foetida* 'Persiana', which was used to breed the world-famous 'Soleil d' Or', the original hybrid of all yellow yard roses.

## American wild roses
Among the most important species are *Rosa virginiana*, Virginia rose, with pale pink blooms followed by plump, spherical, long-lasting hips, and foliage that turns red in fall. *Rosa carolina* and *Rosa nitida* both form vigorous suckers and also change color in fall. *Rosa nutkana* (p. 251) and *Rosa californica* also produce decorative hips.

## Asiatic wild roses
Many forerunners of our modern yard roses came from China and Japan. *Rosa chinensis* and its varieties were, due to their repeat-flowering characteristics, the ancestors of our bedding, hybrid Tea, and repeat-blooming shrub roses. Unfortunately, *Rosa chinensis* is not very hardy. Many of the shrub roses and small shrub roses were developed from *Rosa moyesii* (p. 248) and *Rosa rugosa* (p. 249), while *Rosa multiflora* (p. 247) and *Rosa wichuraiana* (p. 247) produced gorgeous climbers and rambling roses.

# ROSA CANINA
EUROPEAN WILD ROSE / DOG ROSE

**FLOWERING:** Once-flowering; single; Ø 1½–2 in. (4–5 cm.); rose-pink to white; light, fresh wild-rose scent

**GROWTH:** 7–10 ft. (2–3 m.) high; upright; bushy, arching; hooked prickles, also climbs

**HIPS:** From October, orange, smooth, shiny, long, and oval, Ø ¾ in. (2 cm.)

**PLANTING:** Hedges, protection for birds, soil stabilization on banks; maintenance-free

The dog rose blooms in June; its single blooms are initially delicate rose-pink, turning to near white later. They are carried on short stems above pale green, matt foliage and are short-lived. Its hips are long and narrow and, together with the pale yellow fading foliage, look very attractive in fall. The unpretentious dog rose will flourish even on very poor soil. It is much better suited to wild gardens than formal planting. One of its hybrids, 'Kiese', is suitable for use in the yard; its shoots are 7–10 ft. (2–3 m.) long, bearing cherry-red blooms with a white center. *Rosa canina* played an important part in the development of Alba roses. St Mary's Cathedral in Hildesheim, Germany—a UNESCO World Heritage Site—is home to a 1,000-year-old dog rose shrub. Today the dog rose is principally used as rootstock for budding.

◀ The amber-yellow blooms of 'Agnes' no longer reflect its wild-rose ancestry. It is a hybrid with a captivating fragrance. One of its parents is the beautiful double *Rosa foetida* 'Persiana' ('Persian Yellow') from Persia.

# *ROSA RUBIGINOSA*
## SWEETBRIAR, EGLANTINE ROSE / EUROPEAN WILD ROSE

In June, the high point of the rose-blooming season, *Rosa rubiginosa* opens out single, pink blooms that are borne alone or in clusters of up to seven on short, bristly, glandular stems. The calyx, calyx leaves, leaf stems, and especially the leaves are covered with glands, which exude a strong scent of ripe apples particularly in humid conditions or after a storm. Sweetbriar likes limy soil, and is therefore unsuitable for acid, sandy soils. In Great Britain it is used as an ornamental shrub or impenetrable hedging in parks. This rose has contributed greatly to the emergence of yard roses. It gave its apple-scented foliage to the Lord Penzance group of hybrids bred in England. In turn, well-known varieties were bred from this group such as 'Fritz Nobis' (p. 125), 'Magnifica', and 'Hebe's Lip'.

▶ 'Amy Robsart', one of the resistant Penzance hybrids, is once-flowering. The perfume of the magenta-colored blooms combines beautifully with the apple scent of the foliage. This shrub grows to 8 ft. (2.5 m.) and forms scarlet-red hips.

**FLOWERING:** Once-blooming; single; Ø 1¼–2 in. (3–5 cm.); pale pink with creamy-white center; light, fruity, sweet-smelling scent

**GROWTH:** 7–8 ft. (2–2.5 m.) high; vigorous; upright; arching; covered with hooked prickles and bristles

**HIPS:** Scarlet red from October onward; smooth, shiny, oval, Ø ¾ in. (2 cm.)

**PLANTING:** Hedging, protection for birds; stabilization of banks, wild gardens

# ROSA MAJALIS
EUROPEAN WILD ROSE / CINNAMON ROSE, MAY ROSE

**FLOWERING:** Once-flowering; single; Ø 1–2 in. (3–5 cm.); light to carmine pink; light wild-rose scent

**GROWTH:** 5–7 ft. (1.5–2 m.) high; vigorous; upright; bushy; arching

**HIPS:** Dark red; smooth, shiny, spherical, Ø ½ in. (1 cm.)

**PLANTING:** Hedging, protection for birds, stabilization of banks, wild gardens; showy hips

The cinnamon rose tolerates partial shade well and can be found growing wild at the edge of woodland and in riverside forests, where it will even establish itself on poorer soils by forming vigorous suckers. Medieval herbal books quote them as having two forms: once-flowering and repeat-blooming. The latter was later called *Rosa majalis* 'Foecundissima'. It was given the name "May rose" in Germany because of its early blooming period, although this is not until the beginning of June, while the name "cinnamon rose" reflects its brown, often smooth stems. Today this rose, with its dull green, hairy leaves, is occasionally found growing in cottage yards, but it is mainly found in the wild or in wild yards, where it can be used for stabilizing slopes and for hedging.

◀ *Rosa glauca* (red-leafed rose) makes a strikingly attractive-looking yard rose with single, carmine-red blooms and remarkable bluish-mauve frosted foliage.

# *ROSA SPINOSISSIMA*

BURNET ROSE, BIBERNELL ROSE, DUNWICH ROSE / EUROPEAN WILD ROSE

Opinions are divided as to which of the botanic names for the Bibernell or Dunwich rose is more appropriate. The name 'pimpinellifolia' is derived from its seven to nine times divided leaflets that are gray green and finely toothed like those of pimpinellas. In fall they turn bronze red. 'Spinosissima', on the other hand, is the name used to describe the stems, and means "prickliest." This rose, found growing naturally on North Sea coastal dunes, is amazingly unpretentious. It tolerates partial shade and salty soils lacking in nutrients. To find a foothold in the sand, plants growing on their own roots have adapted by forming masses of suckers. The Bibernell rose is already in abundant bloom by the middle of May. The so-called spinosissima hybrids (the spring varieties by Kordes) have inherited this characteristic.

▶ The swelling of the calyx receptacle forms rosehips. They are false and aggregate fruits and the number and size of the seeds in them is specific to the species and variety. *Rosa pimpinellifolia* is adorned with round black fruits.

**FLOWERING:** Once-flowering; single; Ø 2 in. (5 cm.); cream, light yellow or delicate pink; scented

**GROWTH:** 8–78 in. (0.20–2 m.); moderately vigorous; upright to lightly arching; very dense with sharp prickles

**HIPS:** Brownish black; smooth, shiny, round; Ø ¾ in. (2 cm.)

**PLANTING:** For hedges, cover, and protective planting; for wild gardens; heathland gardens

**SYNONYM** *Rosa pimpinellifolia*

# *ROSA FOETIDA* 'BICOLOR'

WILD ROSE FROM ASIA MINOR / CAPUCINE, 'AUSTRIAN COPPER'

**FLOWERING:** Once-flowering; single; Ø 1½–2 in. (4–5 cm.); inside the petals orange red, reverses yellow; unpleasant scent
**GROWTH:** 5–8 ft. (1.5–2.5 m.) high; moderately vigorous; upright; bushy; slender, almost smooth stems
**HIPS:** Brick red; quite bristly; round; Ø ¼ in. (1 cm.)
**PLANTING:** Shrub rose, historic gardens, cottage gardens

Whereas all European and American wild roses come in shades of white, pink, and light red, *Rosa foetida*— 'Austrian briar' from Asia Minor—passed on the long-sought-after yellow color. It was probably brought to Europe as early as the Middle Ages, along with its sport, the Capucine rose (*Rosa foetida* 'Bicolor'). This splendidly colored rose became the ancestor of today's yellow and orange varieties. Unfortunately, together with the special color, it also passed on its susceptibility to black spot. The Capucine rose still delights today; its fiery-colored blooms begin to open early in May; and it has the added curiosity that the blooms sometimes revert to their original yellow color, so that both colors can be seen on a single plant at the same time.

# 'GOLDEN CHERSONESE'

## ONLY VARIETY FROM *ROSA ECAE*, HYBRID OF A WILD ROSE FROM ASIA MINOR

The 39-in. (100-cm.), densely branched wild rose, *Rosa ecae*, was not brought from Afghanistan to Europe until 1880. This is also a species with yellow blooms that are small and single, which open in May or June and look reminiscent of cinquefoil (*Potentilla*). *Rosa ecae* does not make a suitable yard plant, but its only hybrid, 'Golden Chersonese', whose other parent is the shrub rose 'Canary Bird', certainly does. Many of the wild rose characteristics of this once-blooming but abundant variety may still be seen. The flowers emerge all along the long arching stems. This shrub has small delicate foliage and will tolerate shade, which makes it suitable for combining with other plants into a flowering hedge by a fence, planting in front of a fence or wall, or a group of trees.

**FLOWERING:** Once-flowering; single; Ø 2 in. (5 cm.); golden-yellow; light scent

**GROWTH:** 7 ft. (2 m.) high; vigorous; upright to lightly arching; masses of prickles

**HIPS:** Red, pea-size

**PLANTING:** Shrub, for wild gardens

**INTRODUCED:** Allen, 1963, Great Britain

# ROSA MULTIFLORA
ASIATIC WILD ROSE / MULTIFLORA ROSE

*Rosa multiflora* is a strong-growing bundle of energy. This densely branched shrub grows up to 10 ft. (3 m.) high and just as wide. Its small white blooms open out in June or July, carried in large clusters of panicles, followed later by clusters of pea-sized hips. It is a rose that is absolutely ideal for large wild gardens and hedges. This large shrub, introduced from China, has had an enormous influence on our yard roses. Many cluster-flowering shrub roses and numerous large-flowered climbers (such as 'Bobbie James', p. 76, 'Seagull', p. 77, and many others) came from this long-stemmed rose. These easy-to-maintain multiflora climbers were bred at the end of the Victorian age. Their blooming season is four weeks long, they are robust and healthy, and they have comparatively few prickles.

**FLOWERING:** Once-flowering; single; Ø ¾ in. (2 cm.); white; fine, wild-rose scent
**GROWTH:** 5–10 ft. (1.5–3 m.) high; moderately sturdy; arching; branched stems with few prickles
**HIPS:** Red, smooth, shiny, spherical, and pea-sized
**PLANTING:** For hedges; as a specimen shrub in large yards; for cover and protective screening and banks; for wild gardens

▼ *Rosa wichuraiana* also comes from China. Many rambling roses and climbers are descended from this rose, whose blooms are white and do not open until the middle of July. Birds are attracted to their small hips.

# ROSA MOYESII
ASIATIC WILD ROSE

**FLOWERING:** Once-blooming; single; Ø 2–2¾ in. (5–7 cm.); carmine red; no scent

**GROWTH:** 7 ft. (2 m.) high; moderately strong; arching over; rather spindly

**HIPS:** In August/September, orange red; bristles, bottle-shaped; up to 2½ in. (6 cm.) long

**PLANTING:** For hedges, as a specimen; in woodland, attractive to bees, provides protection and food for birds; for wild gardens

Native to Western China, *Rosa moyesii* is rightly considered as one of the most beautiful wild roses. Its crimson blooms with a bright yellow center of large stamens open at the beginning of June at the tips of the small, short secondary branches along the previous year's stem growth. Although they do not possess a scent, they are attractive to insects. The leaves are composed of nine to thirteen delicate, medium green, shiny leaflets. The loosely growing shrub can withstand frost and partial shade; its branches arch decidedly outward so it is best planted as a background setting. Splendid yard varieties, such as 'Geranium', 'Highdownensis', 'Nevada' (p. 101), and 'Marguerite Hilling', have originated from *Rosa moyesii*.

◀ *Rosa moyesii* and its hybrids 'Geranium' and 'Highdownensis' have decorative hips that are beautiful highlights of fall. The orange-red hips are bottle-shaped and up to 2½ in. (6 cm.) long.

# ROSA RUGOSA
## JAPANESE ROSE, RUGOSE ROSE, TURKESTAN ROSE / ASIATIC WILD ROSE

The Japanese Rose (*Rosa rugosa*) comes from the salty sand dunes of Japan and was introduced into Europe in 1796. It is the most frost hardy and salt-tolerant rose, but on calcareous soils it succumbs quickly to iron chlorosis, which turns the leaves yellow; the veins, however, remain green. Many beautiful and robust shrub roses have been bred that show typical Rugosa characteristics: very veined, wrinkled, healthy foliage, along with strong-growing stems that are covered with bristly prickles, and the large scented blooms are carried above the foliage on short stems. After the initial bloom period in June, the occasional bloom may emerge at the same time as the decorative, fleshy hips appear. In fall, *Rosa rugosa* is a real eye-catcher, with its red hips and golden-yellow fall coloring.

▶ 'Dagmar Hastrup' is one of the most well known of the numerous hybrid Rugosas, which make perfect ground cover. This 39-in. (100-cm.) high rose is an abundant repeat bloomer with excellent healthy foliage that turns yellow in fall. Red hips follow the blooms.

**FLOWERING:** Twice-blooming; single; Ø 3½ in. (9 cm.); pink, deep pink, or white; scented

**GROWTH:** 6 ft. (1.8 m.) high; very upright; very densely branched; covered in bristly prickles

**HIPS:** Orange to brick red; smooth, shiny; very round; Ø ¾ in. (2 cm.)

**PLANTING:** For hedges; many varieties make splendid ground cover; as specimens or in groups; for wild gardens

# ROSA XANTHINA FO. HUGONIS
ASIATIC WILD ROSE / GOLDEN ROSE OF CHINA

**FLOWERING:** Once, very
early in the season;
single; Ø 2 in. (5 cm.);
pale yellow
**GROWTH:** 5–8 ft.
(1.5–2.5 m.) high;
moderately vigorous;
broad and bushy; lightly
arching; mature stems do
not have prickles
**HIPS:** Dark maroon to black;
smooth, shiny, oval;
Ø ½ in. (1.5 cm.)
**PLANTING:** Decorative
specimen rose; for wild
gardens

The bright yellow blooms of the elegant Golden Rose of
China have a rarity value among wild roses, and certainly
many have had a sure eye for its beauty. Together with
*Rosa moyesii*, also from China, it is the most frequently
sought-after wild rose. The small, light yellow blooms
begin to open as early as mid-May; they festoon the
short side shoots right along the arching stems. The
splendid blooms of *Rosa xanthina* fo. *hugonis* make the
most impact if planted as a specimen rose in front of a
dark backdrop of trees. It is hardy and also suitable for
dry locations. In very harsh zones it is recommended,
however, to plant the rose on its own roots (not grafted),
as it has been proved that if this is done it is even more
resistant to frost and disease.

◄ *Rosa roxburghii* is a wild rose steeped in ancient
Chinese culture. It bears large, double, scented blooms
on prickly stems, which are followed by round hips
reminiscent of chestnuts.

# ROSA NUTKANA
## AMERICAN WILD ROSE

*Rosa nutkana* is found in the western regions of North America right up to Alaska. It is a loose shrub that is hardy, tolerant of shade, and suckers abundantly on its own roots. Its mauve-pink blooms emerge singly in June or July and are borne right along the stems. Its hybrid, 'Cantab', has even larger blooms. In addition to this rose there are numerous other American wild roses, which, as they were not introduced into Europe until the 18th century or even later, had of all the wild roses very little influence on the breeding of our Modern roses. Some of them, such as *Rosa virginiana*, *Rosa Carolina*, or *Rosa nitida*, not only carry beautiful blooms and hips, but also dazzle in fall with striking red foliage.

**FLOWERING:** Once-blooming; single; Ø 2½ in. (6 cm.); mauve pink; lovely wild-rose fragrance

**GROWTH:** Up to 7 ft. (2 m.); moderately vigorous; very upright; bristly, slender, dark brown stems

**HIPS:** Bright brick red; smooth, shiny; round, Ø ¾ in. (2 cm.)

**PLANTING:** For hedges; as a specimen rose in wild gardens

▶ *Rosa californica* 'Plena' does not offer any fall coloring, but pleases the eye with its clusters of long-lasting blooms, which are succeeded by hips. This densely bushy shrub grows up to 10 ft. (3 m.) high and is best suited as a specimen rose or for hedges.

# INDEX OF ROSES

# USEFUL ADDRESSES

## CANADA

### Canadian Rose Society
c/o Marie Farnady
504-334 Queen Mary Road
Kingston, Ontario K7M 7E7
Tel: 1 613 531 4336
www.canadianrosesociety.org

There are also regional and local societies across the country, including:

### Alberta
Calgary: www.calgaryrosesociety.org
St Albert: www.icangarden.com

### British Columbia
Coquitlam: www.fprosesociety.org
Vancouver: www.vancouverrosesociety.org
Victoria & the Saanich Peninsula: www.nurserysite.com/clubs/peninsular

### Ontario
Barrie: www.huroniarose.usethis.com
Toronto: www.gardenontario.org

### Quebec
www.rosesquebec.org

## UNITED STATES

### American Rose Society
PO Box 30000
Shreveport, Louisiana 71100-0030
Tel: 1 318 938 5402
www.ars.org